*The Student Journalist
and*
DEPTH REPORTING

Communications Supplement

the Lion   May 25, 1967

This is a Lion supplement on communications. Specifically, it is an attempt to relate the observations of Prof. Marshall McLuhan (particularly as they pertain to LT and its students), and to present his approach to interpreting the past and present for the future. The staff hopes that the following will entice the reader into making his own more extensive study of what's happening today, and may tomorrow.

radio	television
lectures	seminars
letters	telephones
written word	spoken word
waltz	improvised dances
monologue	dialogue
phonetic alphabets	hieroglyphics
glasses	sunglasses
pictures	cartoons

Hot and cool media — completely opposed, are causing a cultural revolution.

In McLuhan's land of communications, there exist these two types (with cool predominating). in the modern scene.)

"Hot media are low in participation and cool media are high in participation or completion by the audience," he defines.

Hot excludes — cool includes, involves.

For example, television is cool whereas radio is hot. (But talk-back radio is cooler).

'Understanding Media' . . . memos from McLuhan

Understanding Media is a ledger balancing facts, a chronicle recording human growth from prehistory through the modern electronic era, and a crystal ball offering the reader a preview of the future. It is the highly significant thesis of Marshall McLuhan — a goulash of provocative thinking, down-to-earth facts, and hints at the whys and wherefores of society.

It is difficult to judge whether McLuhan is right or wrong, true or false. He neither moralizes nor preaches; he shows what's happening but doesn't label anything

"good" or "bad." He says, "I neither agree nor disagree with anything I say."

The ideas McLuhan presents are outgrowths of his observations of society. It is a fact that young children watch more television than their parents — McLuhan is not concerned with whether or not watching television is wrong. What is done is not so important as the fact that there is action.

McLuhan is often difficult to read. He does not begin to satisfy the reader who quests for ultimate truths. McLuhan appeals to people who want to know enough to judge for themselves. He says: "There is no theory lurking in my words. I am simply making certain observances so that we can see the forces at work around us."

Understanding Media is a stream of thoughts, rambling through the dark woods of contemporary culture. He explains: "Prose style is noncontinuous — if you tried to talk continuously, you'd drive your listener insane. It's the same with writing. A continuous drone through a book makes it impossible to read. Too

many people try to write and talk like a teletype machine."

Because it is different — because it isn't pure literature, lecture, or almanac — McLuhan excuses **Understanding Media** from the barbs of hostile critics. He says: "I never read my critics. They're essentially concerned with proving their own superiority to the object of their criticism. They don't bother to look around them at his new electronic era, either. In terms of the new media and their effect on the environment, they are illiterate."

behind   the man

We are not faced here by a common, everyday man. We are trying to outline the characteristics of ...

McLuhan, who wrote his first probing ... chemical field ... in 1951 and his most explosive, "Understanding Media," in 1964, has been exploring his environment since he was 22, at Cambridge University, England.

McLuhan is an explorer of life and culture. Some of his material: his Texas-born wife, Corinne, his six children, and himself. His social safari began in 1936 when he arrived to teach freshman classes at the University of Wisconsin.

"I was confronted with young Americans I was incapable of understanding. I felt an urgent need to study their popular culture in order to get through."

Since that time he has engaged in several major projects. He was named director of the Media Project of The National Association of Educational Broadcasters and the U.S. Office of Education in 1959.

He has directed the U. of Toronto's Center for Culture and Technology since 1963.

Following the 1964 publication of "Understanding Media," McLuhan was given the Albert Schweitzer Chair in the Humanities at Fordham University. But the best is yet to come.

THE STUDENT JOURNALIST AND

DEPTH REPORTING

Reporting Issues & Problems in the News

by
BILL G. WARD

Director of Journalism,
Southern Illinois University,
Edwardsville.

RICHARDS ROSEN PRESS, INC., NEW YORK, N.Y. 10010

Standard Book Number: 8239–0251–X
Library of Congress Catalog Card Number: 70–163427

Published in 1972 by Richards Rosen Press, Inc.
29 East 21st Street, New York City, N.Y. 10010

Revised Edition

Manufactured in the United States of America

This book is dedicated to my longtime associates and friends as teachers of scholastic journalism: Tony Cassen, John Reque, Mary Benedict, Norman Moyes, Sam Feldman, Art Levin, Wayne Brasler. And to every teacher confronted by his first deadline: may you, too, be caught up by the excitement and the enthusiasm.

CONTENTS

Frontispiece: The single best piece of work produced by high school journalists in recent years is a special supplement about McLuhan (Marshall). Students at Lyons Township High School in Illinois published it in May, 1967, stimulated by McLuhan's book *The Medium Is the Massage,* to interpret the philosophy and to show how it is part of the school. The front page fold is reproduced here. The other pages are reproduced on pages 54 and 55. The centerfold (map) was printed in two colors. It is reprinted here by permission of the adviser, Miss Kay Keefe. Students on the staff of the supplement were John Steward, Steve Welker, Roberta Novak (art), Karin Randolph (art), Bill Klein, Laird Schaub, Anne Mills, Kathy Van Gunten, Tom Conrad, Nancy Cowan, Barb Benzies, and Carol Taaffe.

*A two-page, packaged depth report about churches—from The Orbit,
John Overton High School, Nashville, Tennessee.*

ABOUT THIS BOOK AND THE AUTHOR

To those of us who have been around newspapers for a quarter century or more, "reporting in depth" seems to be a redundant term. Any reporter worth his by-line should report—without any special urging—in depth. In view of the normal demands for complete facts, balance of opinions, and fairness of presentation, a reporter on every story should be working toward in-depth reporting.

But in the last 10 or 20 years, in-depth reporting has become a genre in itself, considered above and beyond the call of ordinary duty. Maybe it is because our society has been so riddled by sophisticated propaganda and advertising techniques that Truth must be triply underlined. Maybe it is because many reporters in general have become shoddy in their normal, everyday, routine duties. Maybe it is because times have become more complex, and greater effort is needed to get at the complete story. Maybe it is because radio is so shockingly superficial in its news bulletins that they lead invariably to public misunderstanding or disinterest. Maybe television is so powerful in its impact on the reader that—as Vice-President Spiro T. Agnew has suggested—a raised eyebrow or an edge to the voice can unbalance the information. Maybe it is because more reporters are coming from universities with advanced degrees in hand and highly specialized training well beyond the police-blotter and fender-bender level of reporting.

Whatever the reasons, in-depth reporting has become a fashion of journalism in the last two decades—much discussed, carefully studied and coded. Special techniques have been developed and implanted on journalism. Interpretive reporting. Investigative reporting. Analysis. Backgrounding the news. A "situationer." All

9

have moved heavily into the lexicon of journalism. Most newspapers and many magazines list in-depth reporting among their principal responsibilities.

The student press, too. Because most student newspapers are not published daily, they have dropped the straight news story and the event-centered assignment for the more timeless depth report and the issue-centered assignment. WHY and HOW in the news! Not just who, what, when, and where. Student editors refer to the demands of their student audiences as a reason for in-depth reporting. A better reason may be found in the student journalists themselves—better educated, more inquiring, more familiar with reporting techniques. They may be bored intellectually, unchallenged by the routine of most reporting. They may envision so much potential to their reports that they have outstripped teachers and a great many commercial editors who boast of "learning this trade by the seat of my pants."

Those who consistently underestimate our students, for some reason or other, have insisted it takes an adult to do depth reporting. Said one highly successful New York magazine editor to me some years ago, and angrily: "Let students learn how to spell and punctuate. That's about all they can be expected to handle." Well, that attitude and gross misunderstanding of a generation has led to serious conflicts between faculty and students, especially administration and students, and between editors and young reporters.

At Blair Academy in northwest New Jersey ten years ago, a dedicated teacher of journalism thought differently and set out to prove that high school-age students not only can report in depth but in fact should accept the challenge as primary. Perhaps the first high school newspaper in the nation to dedicate itself completely to the news of issues and problems, reported in depth, was the *Blair Breeze* with Tony Cassen as adviser and aggressive and inquisitive students such as Gus Hedberg as editors. The staff of the *Breeze* scoured the East to track down, in full, the stories about youth and politics, youth and the war, youth and the civil-rights movement. Full pages devoted to in-depth stories. Special issues. Writer-photographer teams. Strong opinion sections. The *Breeze* anticipated the turn of student newspapers by about five years.

Well, Tony Cassen believed in in-depth reporting. He believed that the study of journalism should involve seminars in backgrounding contemporary events, in the literature of journalism, in ethics and law. He fitted his philosophy into a six-week summer program and set out to find sponsors. The Newspaper Fund promised support; the trustees and headmaster at Blair promised support and offered encouragement; The Gannett Newspapers, one of the enlightened groups in journalism, joined in heartily with a dozen scholarships. Other newspapers in the East gradually offered support. A great many famous reporters and editors offered their time for special lectures—Jim Hagerty, Stuart Loory, William Kerby, Don Carter. And by the summer of 1964 30 students and six teachers assembled at Blair for a six-week intensified seminar dedicated to the proposition of in-depth reporting and intellectual challenges in journalism. The students exceeded everyone's expectations, and they have built up in colleges reputations and records that are astounding. Tom Hoffman, Tom Dorris, Gus Hedberg, Richard Lampert, Dick Johnson, Tom McCarthy, Cindy Moran, and in the following years such students as Mark Johnson, Rob Wood, Kevin Perrotta, Vashti Smith, Christine George, Harvey Schwartz, Jane Dillinger. The list runs to 200 names or more. They proved the competence of students as in-depth reporters. They proved beyond doubt the value of the Cassen approach to journalism education. And the influence of those students has spread in widening circles for the past decade.

It is only natural that this writer, one of the founding faculty of the Blair summer journalism program, should also be an advocate of in-depth reporting for student journalists. It is from that background and that conviction that this book is produced —as a directive to all students for reporting in depth the persǫns and the events and the problems and the attitudes of their respective schools.

Bill Ward

The author of this book, Bill Ward, has been closely tied to the student press since 1953 when he took his first teaching position at Grove City, Minnesota (English, history, social studies, assistant coach, drama coach, adviser to mimeographed newspaper). Since then he has taught for 15 years in high schools and universities, advised All-American and Pacemaker newspapers and worked with several national award-winning reporters and editors. He has been executive director of the Empire State (New York) Student Press Association. He has written ten books for student journalists. He speaks each year at up to a dozen state, area, and national conferences for student journalists. He has worked for several professional newspapers and has written, all his life, for such publications as *The Christian Science Monitor, The National Observer, The Nation,* and *Camera 35.* He is a firm believer in journalism as literature and in the student newspaper as a leader on campus. He has taught at Syracuse University (with great enjoyment under the inspiration of such fellow professors as Roland Wolseley, Ed Arnold, Wes Clark, Phil Burton), and at the University of Nevada, Reno (a much more conservative and traditional philosophy), and now at Southern Illinois University, Edwardsville, where he is Director of Journalism and founder of the Print program. He is part of a new film-broadcast-print team that is developing a multi-media program for the journalist of the future, one who can use the printed word, the spoken word, and the visual image.

In 1970, Ward was one of 50 educators selected by the National Scholastic Press Association as Pioneers in Journalism for their contributions over the past half century.

A REPORT IN DEPTH

At the Blair Summer School for Journalism for high school students, *Depth Reporting* is the challenge held up to the 16-, 17-, and 18-year-old juniors and seniors from throughout the nation. The *Depth Story*—as the founder of the program Tony Cassen defines it for the student journalists:

A depth story reports the facts in such a way that the reader can FULLY understand them. When you are reporting in depth, you are doing several things, each of which is an element in the story:

You are OBSERVING # You are supplying BACKGROUND INFORMATION # You are HUMANIZING the news # You are INVESTIGATING a situation # You are EXPLAINING what facts really mean # You are ORIENTING the reader # You are ANALYZING or discovering general principles.

Note the word "opinion" is not mentioned. This still belongs on the editorial page. It has no more place in the depth story than in the reporting of straight news.

Each summer since 1964, students have set out to investigate and interpret stories about economy, politics, and environment. Among classes in history and literature and contemporary events —all related to the journalist—students spend part of the five weeks at Blairstown in northwest New Jersey, just across from the Delaware River Gap, digging out the information for depth stories. They learn reporting and writing by meeting from the outset the toughest challenges.

Tom Lewis was one such student in the summer of 1968. He was determined to find out how the Tocks Island Dam Project in that area would affect the small, 200-year-old, conservative com-

13

munities and families in the area. He sought the human factors of a mammoth technological and political project that would change the face of the region.

Here is his report in depth. A student's depth story. The proper place to begin this search into the techniques of depth reporting. Here is the opening challenge for you as a reporter or an editor—as it appeared in the *Blair Reporter*.

For low-cost housing instead of slums, head for the hills.

"Low income housing should be built up in the hills so there won't be any slums," said Mrs. Jack Bielecki, owner of the Empress DriveIn in Blairstown.

Perhaps unknown to Mrs. Bielecki is the fact that if low income housing were to be built in most of the land areas around Blairstown, it would have to be built "up in the hills," if at all, due to the subdivision policies of the township committees in this area.

An influx of low income workers into the Blairstown area has, according to officials of the Tocks Island Regional Advisory Committee, already begun at a slow pace. The speed of this influx is expected to increase rapidly, culminating in either 1976 or 1977 with the completion of the Tocks Island Dam Project and the Delaware Water Gap National Recreation Area (DWGNRA).

The DWGNRA is expected to account for an estimated 10.5 million visitors and vacationers a year, plus a projected one billion dollar's worth of new industries and services coming into a seven-county area in the states of New Jersey, New York, and Pennsylvania. The counties affected in New Jersey will be Sussex and Warren Counties.

These new services and industries will require workers to staff them. Throughout the period between now and 1977, a steady growth of new enterprises will occur. After a few years, a new influx of businesses is expected to begin after others have seen the probable success of the businesses already servicing the DWGNRA.

This second group of industries and services will also require new workers to staff them. The unemployment percentage in the Blairstown area is practically negligible. It is without any doubt insufficient to provide anywhere near the number of "employables" that will be needed.

Thus, according to TIRAC officials and state leaders such as John W. Gleeson, director of the New Jersey Office of Community Services, a migration of low income workers will have to take place to fulfill this labor market demand.

A logical question to ask is, "Where are all these people going to live?" The answer is not a simple one. In fact, the answer's complexities delve deep into the behaviors of the people already established in this area.

In most of the townships of this area, notably Blairstown Township and Frelinghuysen Township, no land tracts have been designated as areas for the development of low income housing. In Blairstown Township, the majority of potential subdivisions are similar to one called Silver Lake. In Silver Lake, a developer may sell lots no smaller than three-fourths of an acre in size. The available land left in Frelinghuysen Township is sold in lots no smaller than one or two acres in size.

"Low income families cannot afford to buy land at prices ranging from $4000–$8000 an acre and then put a house on it," said Robert Swetnam of the Blairstown Insurance Agency. His statement reveals the key to the fact that low income people are effectively barred from settling in much of this area.

But, according to TIRAC and state officials, low income people will be migrating into this area because of the increased labor market to be provided by the DWGNRA. Thus, a solution, or solutions, must be found to accommodate these people upon their arrival.

According to Gleeson, industry and business realize the lack of employables in this area. Thus, he continued, in many cases new industry will offer to settle in an area and provide tax revenue if in return the township will build a substantial number of low income dwellings to provide living space for new employees.

Gleeson cited as one example an industry that offered to settle in the Montclair, N. J., area. The industry was taxable for over $800,000 a year, but it insisted that 500 low income houses be built to accommodate employees. Its offer was accepted.

Such a system of procuring low income housing might be effective in a township like Frelinghuysen, but in a township like Blairstown it would prove ineffective. Blairstown Township enjoys a special situation. The nearly $1 million in tax revenues it receives from the Yard's Creek Pumped Storage Plant of New Jersey Power and Light Company almost entirely pays for the township's expenses. Thus, bargains with industry are not needed, even to supplement the township's budget.

In situations such as this, Gleeson believes that it is possible that new towns may spring up to absorb these people. Also, he said, developers and speculators might buy up large tracts of farm lands and then try to influence the local planning committees into allowing low income houses to be built on those sites.

Gleeson and Swetnam both feel, however, that intervention by higher authorities would occur before new towns would ever spring up. The Delaware River Basin Commission, a regional organization, has such power to set aside lands for low income housing developments. Also, according to Swetnam, the federal government may intervene under the constitutional right of eminent domain and set up federal housing projects in this area.

Thus, it seems that despite the local government's attitudes toward low income housing, the building of such housing is inevitable. It is important to remember, however, that local officials in rural communities tend to very closely reflect the attitudes of their constituency. This would seem to indicate, then, that the residents of this area harbor adverse feelings toward low income housing and low income people.

Jean Paul Richter of the New Jersey Council of Churches emphasized in a recent public appearance that racial viewpoints in the Blairstown area need a "strong liberalization." This statement would seem to indicate that he sees a prejudice on the part of the people of this area against minorities, Negroes and Puerto Ricans in particular, who generally compose the majority of the low income bracket.

The Rev. Mr. Wesley Crowther of the First Presbyterian Church in Blairstown states, "We have basically in this particular area what might be called a rather strong, even extreme right wingism." He continued, "There are so few (Negroes) in this community that there is, shall I say, an unconscious fear. I think in the absence of Negro people . . . possibly many of the people who have never really rubbed elbows with them (Negroes), any time in their long lives, have built up an unconscious fear."

The Rev. Mr. Crowther seems to have hit the basic stumbling block to the building of low income housing in this area. Historian Richard Hofstadter has termed it "negrophobia," or a fear of Negroes and generally of people not in the same social bracket.

This "negrophobia" may be a disease within people in the area which in turn manifests itself in the actions of their local governments. Thus, it appears necessary that external power structures will have to take the steps needed to procure low income houses.

Certainly, under the existing system of high-priced, large lots as the minimum sale, people with low incomes cannot afford to purchase homes. Yet, these people will come despite the attempts of the local power structures to keep them out.

These local power structures reflect the prejudice and aversion to change that can be found within the people. Therefore, it seems all but inevitable that action will have to be taken within the next few years by the Delaware River Basin Commission and the federal government to ensure homes for the people involved in the influx of labor inherent in the Delaware Water Gap National Recreation Area project.

"The reader (believes) that he is going to find out what is going on in the world; and it does not seem to me that the newspaper is giving him his money's worth if it only gives him what somebody says is going on in the world, with no hint as to whether what that somebody says is right or wrong."

—Elmer Davis
Columnist, commentator.

Chapter I

THE NEW DIMENSIONS OF STUDENT JOURNALISM

By 1967 a dozen high school newspapers across the nation had shifted news priorities toward the depth story. College editors were swinging mightily at issues and problems, ignoring much spot news. Advisers such as John Reque, Wayne Brasler, Mary Benedict, and Art Levin were encouraging students to a more vigorous, more serious, and much more demanding kind of journalism. They were quickly joined by advisers and teachers from one coast to the other. And most new advisers to join the ranks in the late 1960's and early 1970's were, by nature, dedicated to depth stories.

What were they teaching and the editors doing? Some persons equated depth stories with opinion matter. Wrong! Some explained depth reporting by contrasting it with straight news stories. Not very definitive! Some depth reporters such as Mark Arnold of the depth-conscious *National Observer* characterized it this way: "What you do is place the event into a wider perspective." A television newsman called it "comprehensive news reporting."

Eric Sevareid, another television newsman, explained, "It's not offering an opinion as much as taking a broader look at events. . . . We're caught up in automation and escalation and population. Every viewer can't know all the news. Today it has become the reporter's job to tell the public what will happen 'if' and 'when.' "

Sevareid was firm. "The facts don't mean a thing unless they can be translated to carry across the full impact of a situation."

19

News needing detailed explanation: The Ecumenical Council, Job Corps, farm surplus, and escalation. National debt, silent majority, credibility gap, and Astro-Turf. Great Society, protective reaction bombing, geodesic dome. Depression, inflation, and planned unemployment.

State of the Nation?
Taxation vs. inflation:
        Which way?
As for Vietnam:
Escalation or negotiation,
Or to some evacuation,
                How about pacification?
(Well, at least cessation.)
For Congress: peroration;
At least, mesmerization
        of the masses.
The opposition claims misinformation,
outright fabrication,
even hallucination
        on The Hill.
The party-in-power claims
Most logical calculation,
        of course.
For schools: integration.
For politics: 3rd partyization.
For the Pentagon: powerization
As the answer to vexation.
Billy Graham: salvation,
        by all means.
Ex-Presidents: memoirization.
Youth: revitalization
                of the nation.
                Or:
hallucinations at The Pad.

TV: spectacularization.
Wall Street: speculation
followed by frustration
and considerable damnation.
And for reporters! the moral
is plain to see!
Interpretation.

Reporter Mark Arnold makes the point once again about reporting in depth: "A reporter's job is to inform and if he does the job fully he must tell the reader not just what a budget increase amounts to but what it means *to him*."

When tuition and fees were raised at the University of Nevada, Reno, student reporter Sue De Berry was not satisfied with a fact-based story announcing the amount of increase, its date of effectiveness, and what the Board of Regents said at the meeting where it was voted into effect. The student merited more information than that, especially since the increase would force many students —economically prostrate already—out of college. So she began to widen the report and to dig below the surface.

Why, according to the Regents, was the increase necessary?

Rise in cost of living (the facts, please, about that).
Increase in bank interest (what?).
Rise in construction costs.
Increase in salaries.

Who has authority to assess increases? Where was the decision made, by whom, exactly when?

All fees are subject to change by the Board of Regents.
The catalog promises students, ". . . keep the fees as low as possible."

How do the fees compare in the region, and nationally?

The college is now among the top 10 state colleges in tuition costs.

What is the *reaction* of students?

Twenty-five percent had never heard of the increase.
Some will transfer elsewhere.
Most have to find extra funds somewhere.
Most say the increase is fine if it expands the University. Most would stay—and pay.

Where would the additional money really go?

Health service.
Building program.
No one knows exactly.

Why the especially heavy increase for nonresident students?

One administrator: "It acts as a deterrent for nonresident growth."

All of this—and more—goes into a story in depth. The reader begins to understand WHY and HOW as well as exactly WHAT.

Other student reporters asked more WHY and HOW questions to try to find out the significance of *the causal factors for, the potential effects of, the real reasons for* situations and problems and events on campus.

Why the demise of college boxing?—The death of boxer Charlie Mohr at Wisconsin most of all. Mohr died in 1960; a year later three fourths of the college teams had disbanded. . . .

Football is more dangerous as a sport, but boxing has a bad name associated with gangsters.

Why and how the change in image of school security police? Need more college-educated officers who understand colleges and students . . . more special training . . . change the trappings of a policeman to the blazer-and-trousers of "law enforcement officers" . . . preventive measures stressed.

What is life like for foreign students?

The extent of drugs on campus—and reasons for the increase in usage?

All of this, student journalists began to realize, must go into news reporting if a newspaper or news magazine is going to perform any useful function on the campus. As a writer declared in an article in *Fortune* magazine (itself a pioneer in depth reporting as far back as the 1930's):

> Today every public question—national defense, water pollution, educational policy—involves highly specialized kinds of knowledge. The citizen cannot be adequately informed unless his education and, later, his journalism give him some access to that essential part of a public question that lies outside his own immediate sphere of interest and competence.

Max Ways continued in the article to make another key point about the movement from fact-centered stories to interpretive stories and other kinds of news in depth:

> . . . the loosening of parental authority or the increase of consumer credit or public acceptance of a new technology of contraception, the rising resentment of black Americans are much more difficult to pinpoint. They are not "events." They didn't happen "yesterday" or "today" or "last week." They do not fit the journalist's cherished notions of a "story."

For examples of popular publications that explained the news as well as reported its instant facts, he referred to *The Christian Science Monitor, The Wall Street Journal, Time* and *Newsweek* magazines, and the basically unknown quarterly *Daedalus*.[1]

Reporting in depth has not been accepted with unanimous enthusiasm. As high school and college newspapers more and more have added "depth" to their guidelines, they have encountered reluctance as frequently as acceptance. For one thing, those who make news usually prefer that only *their* viewpoints be publicized. Opposition silenced! Reasons must not be subjected to scrutiny! The decision made and announced and applied! That is one reason President Richard Nixon in the early years of his administration complained so bitterly about his speeches and news releases being subjected to evaluation and depth reporting.

If a person or an institution can set policy unchallenged, then the people have no rights at all to participation in decision-making.

Thus, depth reporting usually goes beyond the convenient set announcements made by a policy-making entity. And there is antagonism sometimes from those who must then defend and/or rationalize said policies.

One commercial newspaper identifies its depth stories by an inset headline "Probe." A college paper refers to "Perspective."

Whatever—it is essentially honest, detailed, aggressive, responsible and objective reporting, intended to give the reader as much information about all sides of the news so that (1) he can understand more of what happens, (2) he can make more intelligent decisions if called upon, and (3) he can live more in a world of intelligent direction.

It is no surprise that since 1964, as high school and college students have become more participatory, they have turned en-

---

[1] *Fortune,* October 1969, page 110.

thusiastically in their journalism to opinion matter and depth reporting.

To Do, to Read, to Think About

1. Television correspondent David Schoenbrun talking to student journalists about the necessity for a higher level of journalism:

"Americans need to be informed about many things, especially the Vietnam war. We have been told that we are honoring a treaty, but no one has seen or read the treaty because there isn't one. . . .

"We are abusing the United Nations Charter and no one has mentioned that the United States was obliged by the charter to come before the U.N. before going into Vietnam. This we did not do. When the talk of treaties came up, not one journalist questioned it. I think journalists have forgotten what their job is. They should be watchmen, looking out for danger and ready to spread the alarm if there is any. . . .

"Everyone wants 'good news' but when you go to a doctor you don't want only the good news. You want to know where the trouble is so it can be cured. Journalists, too, must diagnose the trouble so we can do something about it."

Here is Samuel G. Blackman, for 42 years a newspaperman and general news editor of the Associated Press (1958–1969), quoted just before retirement:

"No longer can newspapers be content to report just the surface events of the day—the accidents that befall us on land, sea, and air; the debates in legislative halls; the rulings of courts of law; or statistics on capital spending and employment. Newspapers must relate these to their readers and their daily lives. They must report and explain the myriad changes that occur in the makeup of societies everywhere in the world.

". . . Our garden is a world filled with dangers, made more so by the proliferation of nuclear weapons. New discoveries in space, medicine, communications, transportation, and in count-less other areas dazzle mankind. The complexity of the world de-mands that newspapers do more backgrounding, interpreting, and explaining than ever before—in other words, putting flesh on the bare bones of the news.

"In experimenting on an expanded approach to the news—the news analysis is one such approach—newspapers must not be afraid to make innovations, even though they make some mis-takes. Thomas Edison was once asked why he kept trying to make a new type of battery when he had failed often. He replied: 'Fail-ure? I have no failures. Now I know 50,000 ways it won't work.'

"The late Bernard Kilgore, who made *The Wall Street Journal* into one of the nation's outstanding newspapers, once said, 'The newspaper editor of tomorrow will be an egghead. The newspa-per of the future must become an instrument of education lead-ership, an instrument of intellectual development—a center of learning.'

"I envy those who are about to become newspapermen and newspaperwomen. I wish I were twenty-one. . . ."

Those two quotes provide the basis for first thoughts and dis-cussions about reporting in depth and its value to both commer-cial and student press.

2. Are there controversial issues and problems that the stu-dent press must stay out of? For some student staffs, the war in Vietnam has been declared out-of-bounds. For some, curriculum, teachers, and policy. For some, any negative news that supposedly tarnishes the image of the school, whether the news (and the image) is true or not.

3. For more familiarity with depth stories, read in *The Chris-tian Science Monitor, The National Observer, Time, Newsweek,* and *Harper's.*

4. Check with local newspapers and broadcast newsmen for anyone who specializes in depth reporting. He should be asked to meet with staff or class at the earliest opportunity. He can give

a firsthand overview of the problems, perils—and pleasures—of reporting in depth.

5. For television, several programs are really depth reports: white papers, special documentaries, "magazine" shows such as *60 Minutes*. Watch television listings for them and be sure to observe and analyze them for reporting techniques, topic definitions, and successes and failures.

A DEPTH STORY TO STUDY

This section was opened with a story in depth, by a student, about the noncampus world. To show how the commercial journalist handles a story in depth about the campus world, here is a report about: "Does the potential of injuries outweigh values of scholastic athletics?" It comes from the wires of the Associated Press, October 11, 1969.

Subsequent depth stories will be critiqued systematically. This one, however, is to be read in its entirety so that you can get the "sense" of mood, purpose, and techniques of *reporting in depth*. Study it carefully for content. Ask yourself how the reporter got each segment of his information.

Are Sports Worth It?

NEW YORK, Oct. 11 (AP)—Suddenly the cheering stops, players gather in a circle around an injured comrade, then part to make way for the stretcher.

It's a scene re-enacted countless times each autumn when high school football gets under way.

While the number of accidents appears to be on the decline and the severity of injuries is decreasing, athletic injuries to youths continue to cause concern.

The concern is heightened when, as occasionally happens, one of the youngsters dies.

There are no nationwide statistics available on the number of injuries actually suffered each year by youthful athletes, but fatalities directly resulting from athletic injury are tabulated. In the latest available year, 1967, there were 16 deaths among high school football players.

In the same year, three college and five sandlot players died. There were no deaths among professional or semiprofessional players.

Medical authorities, educators and coaches maintain that the benefits gained far exceed the risk of serious injury.

"More harm is done by excluding kids from physical competition than from allowing it for kids not fit for it," Dr. Eugene Diamond, professor of pediatrics at Loyola University, Chicago, said recently.

Speaking at a course on athletic injuries sponsored by the American College of Surgeons, Dr. Diamond said, "The rare sudden deaths are due to poor training practices or rare disorders not easily detected."

Only eight states have insurance programs covering athletes, and only three of these have comprehensive insurance programs. These states are the source of such injury statistics as are available because records must be kept for claims purposes.

Even these statistics are incomplete. They include only injuries serious enough to require medical attention and insurance compensation. Also, many boys will not report to their coaches minor injuries for fear they will be kept out of play.

The reliability of statistics in fatalities also is sometimes questioned. It is not always certain that a death is caused directly by an athletic injury. It could result from a pre-existing condition that the player's coach, and the player, did not know about.

On the other hand, there is sometimes a tendency on the part of team physicians to blame pre-existing ailments rather than the injury because such fatal injuries create considerable parental and public concern over the safety of organized sports.

Wisconsin has one of the three comprehensive insurance programs.

Records maintained by the Wisconsin Interscholastic Athletic Association show that football leads in that state as the cause of injury.

Wisconsin State has about 6,000 compensable claims a year resulting from football injuries among the 36,000 football players covered. The figures are about 2,000 for basketball, 2,000 for wrestling, 700 for track and 300 for baseball.

But the number of participants and the time devoted to an activity must be considered also. For a four-year period, for example, fatality statistics in relation to each 100,000 participants showed college and high school football averaged 3.9 a year.

Clifford Fagan, executive secretary of the National Federation of State High School Athletic Associations, said that generally one out of every five high school football players will be injured seriously enough for insurance compensation.

There are about 975,000 boys who play high school football each year.

Fagan said the number and extent of athletic injuries is declining, in large measure because of improved equipment.

In 1948, he said, injuries to the head, face, and neck area accounted for 52 percent of all injuries reportable and that these now account for about 20 percent.

Dental injuries are now negligible, he said, because boys playing football are required to wear mouth protectors, as well as face masks.

Starting in 1971, the length of the cleat worn on football shoes will be a half inch, compared with seven-eighths inch in the past.

It is expected that this will reduce knee injuries, the No. 1 injury in football. It has been found that the shorter cleat gives the player more maneuverability and that he does not "dig in" the turf with his foot.

There also have been several experiments and improvements in football helmets. Ohio State University uses foam rubber helmets now.

Head injuries are the No. 2 cause of injuries in high school football.

"We do believe we have a great responsibility in making games as safe as we can," Fagan said.

He described some of the improved equipment as a mixed blessing in that it sometimes gives the player a feeling of false security and he takes more risks.

With the face mask, he noted, the player now "puts his head in the meat grinder"—that is, he places his head in the chest of his opponent and holds it there. This can result in spinal damage that is not immediately detectable, and it is suspected that it may contribute to arthritic conditions.

The minor bruises, sprains and strains of athletics "are a part of growing up," said Fagan, a former high school coach. If overly protected, the boy will grow up with fear he should not have, he said.

The biggest problem in prep football is that the man on the street and sometimes the educator wants these players to use the same tactics as professionals, Fagan said.

Fagan said, "The pride of the community should not rest on the team, but on education."

Unless school sports are used for education, eventually the sport suffers, he said.

In a recent issue of Medical Tribune, Dr. Kenneth D. Rose of the University of Nebraska wrote that there were 44 heart-related deaths in organized sports at all levels between 1961 and 1967.

Of these, 38 victims were between 14 and 19 years old. And, he said, 36 of the 41 football deaths were in preseason practice.

Dr. Rose wrote: "The vicious practice of 'deliberate spearing' (blocking or tackling the opponent with the helmeted head) not only leads to alarmingly high incidence of head and neck injuries in the blocker, but occasional cardiac contusion in the person blocked . . .

"Unfortunately, and in spite of disclaimers by the coaching profession, the technique of spearing is taught at all levels of football, from midget to professional," he said.

Dr. G. Lawrence Rarick of the University of California told the American Medical Association's National Conference on Medical Aspects of Sports in Miami Beach that "exploitation of children to satisfy the whims of overly ambitious parents, coaches, and community boosters" is one of the controversial issues in sports.

"Herein lies a real threat to the welfare of youth," he said.

Professional players often are called on to set a good example for their young fans and emulators.

For example, an editorial in the AMA Journal implored professional ice hockey players to wear helmets as encouragement to young players to do the same.

This followed the deaths of a pro hockey player and two Canadian youths from head injuries when playing the game without helmets.

Basketball injuries generally have no lasting effect, Fagan said, and generally are sprains and bruises. There are relatively few broken bones.

Wrestling is the fastest growing sport in high school, he said, and causes few broken bones, most of the injuries being abrasions and dislocations.

Fagan termed "alarming" the rate of serious injuries in sandlot football. This comes about from lack of supervision, mismatching of opponents and ill-fitting equipment, he said.

He added that poor-fitting equipment sometimes is worse than none at all because it hinders a boy from protecting himself.

The percentage of injuries in elementary school football is "surprisingly low," Fagan said. He suggested that this might be because of the small size and lack of strength of the young players.

But Fagan, like other authorities, opposes high-pressure interscholastic competition for these youngsters.

Reprinted by permission
of the Associated Press

FIVE DEPTH STORY IDEAS

1. How seriously are students at your school, on your campus, directly affected by environmental pollution?

2. In what ways—according to present evidence—will your school be different in 1984?

3. Is "free public education" really free as far as the student himself is concerned?

4. In the search for new and better methods of education— whether instruction or learning—what within the last 10 years has been tried for the first time and already been dropped or rejected as unsuccessful?

5. How does the availability of federal funds—or lack of them, depending upon appropriations for the year—directly affect your school? Where do those funds show up, with what end results that the student can see, hear, or feel?

#

"It is no longer enough to report the fact truthfully. It is now necessary to report the truth about the fact."

—Commission on Freedom of the Press, 1947.

"You cannot merely report the literal truth. You have to explain it."

—James B. Reston
Columnist, New York Times.

Chapter II

WHY THE STORY IN DEPTH?

Truth is buried deep. What lies near the surface may not be truth, as much as "simplism." What is easy to arrive at is more convenience than validity. And a journalist early in his career must arrive at a decision about this matter, "truth." To get to it demands energy, time involvement, and an unrelenting dedication.

For instance: what about dress codes in high schools? They have been under severe criticism in recent years and in many schools have undergone extensive surgery. One school in the Chicago area outlaws in class inner garments worn as outer garments, bathing suits, and gym clothes. Nothing else is prohibited. Other schools proscribe a long list of apparel. But to arrive at the truth about controversial dress codes, you must examine a variety of details:

(1) What is the purpose of the codes, as interpreted by many persons or groups of persons? The "why?"

(2) When did the local code originate and for what reasons? What are dress codes in other schools?

(3) How has the local code changed during the years, and why?

(4) What are the legalities? Can students by law be forced to conform to codes that may impose hardship on them? Outlaw Levis and you may drive some low-income students from the school.

(5) What are all the proposed changes—and what are the supporting arguments?

(6) What are the preferences of students, of faculties, of administration?

(7) What would happen in the school if the present code were changed significantly?

(8) Exactly what does the present code say? Exactly what punishments—and how many—have been assessed? Is the code enforced?

(9) How much is the code symbolic? A school board member opposes changes because he thinks it will benefit "long hair" and he associates long hair with sin, or communism, or deviant behavior. In any such case, he stands against a symbol.

Those nine points lead to reporting the news story in depth. They take the reporter far beyond the superficial and simplistic, as represented by these conclusions.

√ A change would mark a breakdown in law and order and would challenge the authority of school boards and administrators to make decisions.

√ Short haircut means solid citizen; long hair means anarchist.

√ Tradition must prevail, simply because it is what always has been done; the reactionary attitude that change must be resisted because it is—change.

And so on!

Therefore, a depth story is a complete, precise, and even exhaustive report about a contemporary event, idea, or situation of interest and importance to the reader. It is thorough reporting. It is smooth, clear, and interesting writing. It is the peak of accomplishment that reporters strive for. Before the reader/citizen can make an intelligent decision he must know all the facts, all the significant viewpoints, the historical perspective, and the projected "causes and effects."

It is possible that the greatest controversy of modern America, the involvement in the war in Vietnam, resulted from incomplete information—if not misinformation. Where is Vietnam? What is its strategic importance to Americans? What is its history as a political entity? What are the several forces in competition in Vietnam? Who (and why) are the important personalities involved—Ho Chi Minh, Diem, Ky? What are the religious implications, the ethnic conflicts? To understand American involvement in Vietnam in the escalating years of 1965 and 1966, American citizens needed information *in depth* from newspapers and television. They did not get it, but instead mostly propaganda reported from the military, the President's office, and certain Vietnamese political forces. Unable to make important decisions on the basis of full and complete and truthful information, Americans turned in ignorance and fear to simple solutions that "seemed" to fit preconceptions:

- Contain communism, protect capitalism.
- Fight "there" to avoid warfare "here."
- Avenge the death of Americans sent to Vietnam to fight the war.
- Follow the flag, or advocate the slogan "Love It or Leave It."
- Support the decisions of your President; he is the only one you've got.
- To oppose the war is traitorous. Or, to support the war is foolhardy.

And so on!

For years, Americans at home divided into philosophic camps and fought the war on simplisms and superficialities—mainly because the mass media failed to give full, complete, in-depth, truthful information. Mainly, the press reported what the governments in Saigon and Washington claimed. Propaganda mostly designed to prove the incumbent powers indisputably right and successful.

Therefore, reporting in depth supports an open and free society. It scarcely can be tolerated in a closed and repressive society.

Depth reporting is honest reporting.

It is industrious and meticulous reporting.

It is unbiased reporting.

It demands time, money, and manpower. It rates as the higher performance. It is the product of journalism working from the intellect as well as the viscera.

For journalists there is the problem of individuals' receiving fragments of information so that there is no cohesive whole.

"Hear the students are up on campus demonstrating."

Without further information to provide a fuller picture, the receiver of partial information fills in with bias, his preconceived ideas, and his knowledge of similar past experiences. He puts the fragment into his own "context"—and his perception may be totally wrong. Yet it will be difficult for him to change, or for someone else to correct him. His "conclusions" will seem logical to him.

Back to the proposed change in the school's dress code. What if the code calls for restrictions impossible to comply with—because of fashion changes? (Code: "Boys at all times must wear belts with trousers." Trousers no longer provide belt loops.) Then the emotional argument of a board member, "These kids just want to get away with something, and it's my job to see that they don't!" won't be consistent with the facts. To report the board member's opinion without the countering facts of the style changes leads to confusion and misunderstanding. It leads to an emotional reaction by the public instead of a rational one.

A pro-war leader who insists that all anti-war protestors are drug addicts and anarchists must be reported in his quotes along with an honest description of the crowd at a protest meeting. In the crowd may be laborers, white-collar workers, teachers, and doctors. To allow the emotional charge of one person to stand without investigating its truthfulness is to involve all citizens in unworthy decisions based upon one-sided charge and evidence. It is lending the Press to every strident demagogue who wants to use it for his own malevolent purposes.

The student press has turned in recent years more and more to depth reporting, and has devoted less and less attention to "bulletin board" news. Some examples:

• Feeling that an important bond issue had been insufficiently presented to the voters of the district, editors of *The Proviso Profile* of Maywood, Illinois, developed a two-page special issue covering the proposal in depth. It was circulated to parents/voters.

• Desiring high school students to know more about current events, editors of the *Central High Tiger* of Little Rock, Arkansas, in every issue devoted a full page to in-depth coverage: highway safety, the first-year performance of the new governor, youth juries, integration of the high school. Whenever a confusing or emotional issue hit the campus at Kent State University, Ohio, editors produced a four-page, in-depth study called "Perspective."

• Certain that students misunderstand many of the innovations in education—modular scheduling, team teaching, noncognitive approaches—the editors of *The Blueprint* at Ramsey High School in Minnesota produced a full 12-page issue about the Three Modern R's.

The subjects for special in-depth reporting have been varied. Jogging to lose weight. The disappearing circus. Environmental pollution. Women's liberation movement. Youth air fares. Maxiskirts. Increase in popularity of specialized magazines. Student rights. Skiing fanatics. For every daily edition of *The Wall Street Journal,* the best guide to depth reporting, at least three such topics are explored, generally on page 1. Politics, culture, fashions and fads, economics, education—all aspects of life and society are vulnerable to depth reporting.

All in the interest of truth, not just facts-reporting. All in the desire for complete information to set before the reader. All in the hopes of a more intelligent society making more rational decisions.

Depth reporting is the counterattack on propaganda, intentional falsehood, and personal gain through misinformation. In

January 30, 1970   LITTLE ROCK CENTRAL HIGH TIGER   Page 7

Blacks Contribute Much To Society

By CHERIE JOHNSON

Traditional American history texts tend to overlook some of the significant aspects of the role of the black man.

The Little Rock School District is presently trying to present in its history courses a more accurate account of the story of this nation, giving attention to the contributions and influences of the largest minority group in the country, the Afro-American.

Bring Culture

The Africans who were brought to the New World were not without a history. The uniquely African culture they brought became part of the American heritage, while remaining the special heritage of the Afro-American.

Afro-American contributions to the growth and development of the nation were numerous and valuable. However, the black man could have perhaps made greater contributions had it not been for severe political, social, and economic restrictions.

During the course of slavery, blacks revolted under the leadership of such people as Harriet Tubman, Toussaint L'Overture, and Demark Vesey. Another freedom fighter was Sojourner Truth.

Turner Leads

The South was never the same after the insurrection led by Nat Turner, the black prophet, in 1831. Turner, who claimed he saw visions and was commanded by God, led a revolt to free Virginia from slavery.

In the course of 48 hours his band swept across Southhampton County and in the process killed approximately 55 whites. The band was finally dispersed and eventually Turner and his conspirators were hanged. However, the fear that he and his men caused lived on. Never again did the slave owner feel comfortable.

Blacks Contribute

Since the end of slavery, there have been many black men to arise and contribute much to the Negro race and humanity as a whole.

The National Association for the Advancement of the Colored and has since been instrumental in the cause of gaining the rights of blacks.

One of the founders of the NAACP and an opponent of Booker T. Washington's philo-

KALO Programs 'Profiles in Ebony'

Does the name Chrispus Attucks or Mary McLeod Bethune ring a bell? If not, listening to radio station KALO will alleviate this silent unfamiliarity.

Throughout the day, KALO presents a brief program that is intended to make its listeners more aware of the Afro-American contributions to our society.

This program, entitled "Profiles in Ebony," reflects the lives and achievements of blacks who might otherwise be ignored by history texts.

"Profiles in Ebony" can be heard at one hour intervals from the station's sign-on to sign off.

Information used in the broadcast is donated by the Johnson's Publications Company.

sophy of Negro education that emphasized vocational training was W. E. B. Dubois. He was also the first black to receive a PhD degree from Harvard.

Marshall Advances

Thurgood Marshall, a graduate of Howard University, served as a lawyer on the NAACP Legal Defense Fund beginning in 1935.

He presented the NAACP case in the precedent-setting 1954 case of Brown vs. the Board of Education, which ordered an end to school segregation. Marshall is now a U. S. Supreme Court Justice.

Probably best known for contributions to humanity is the late Rev. Martin Luther King, Jr. King was a prime force in the desegregation of numerous Southern institutions.

Gets Nobel Prize

Because of his efforts to promote racial harmony, King was presented the Nobel Peace Prize in 1964. He was one of the founders of the Southern Christian Leadership Conference presently headed by the Rev. Ralph Abernathy, his successor.

Black accomplishments do not stop at freedom fighters. There have been scientists and writers, musicians and entertainers, and bankers and businessmen who have gained national prominence.

George W. Carver discovered many ways of using such simple plants as peanuts and soy beans; Dr. Charles Drew is responsible for finding a way to store blood plasma in blood banks.

And, there are others, including present day militants Eldridge Cleaver and Stokley Carmichael, who follow the traditions of Malcolm X.

L'Overture   Truth   Washington   King

Macolm X   Abernathy   Carmichael   Cleaver

Issue of the Issue

Nation's Blacks Review History

'Blacks Face Many Problems,' Says Prominent Local Attorney

By CHERIE JOHNSON

"Black people have been faced with every type of problem imaginable since the beginning of slavery to the present day."

These were the words of Eldridge Cleaver and Stokley Carmichael, a prominent Little Rock attorney who specializes in civil rights cases.

Reveals Problem

"The greatest problem that the black man has faced is his systematic exclusion from government participation," Mr. Walker said, adding that this exclusion was directly responsible for many of the other problems.

He indicated that 25 per cent of Little Rock's population is composed of blacks "Therefore, 25 per cent of government positions should have been held by blacks," he said.

The attorney feels the "system" permits a few "show piece Negroes" that can be pointed out as "shining examples" of what black people can do under white leadership.

Attacks Tokenism

"Tokenism, in general, is designed to keep the vast majority of blacks satisfied," Mr. Walker said. "What it all boils down to is the system appears fair, but it really isn't."

Discussing education, Mr. Walker noted that when schools are integrated, it is usually the formerly all-white school that remains open while the all-black school is closed.

"Does this mean the all-black school is inferior to the white school when all our schools are supposedly equal in educational quality?" Walker asked.

Cites Challenge

In the next decade, Mr. Walker cited "mere survival" as most challenging for Negroes.

"Even though blacks have somehow managed to survive, there still is a systematic effort being made to destroy black images," he said. He indicated that "brainwashing of blacks by whites" sets blacks apart from other blacks.

Mr. John Walker

"What we need," the attorney said, "is to have more unity among the members of our race."

Sees No Solution

According to Mr. Walker, there are no "real solutions" to racial problems immediately available.

However, he indicated that if blacks were put into positions of leadership, it would hasten the solution to the problems.

"Whites don't know what black needs are, so how can they enact into law what is best for us?" he asked.

"Progress has been made but we have a long way to go yet," he said.

Group Promotes Black History, Culture; Asks for 'Understanding Between Races'

"Understand Your Brother." These meaningful words are the motto for a newly organized organization of approximately 200 students who call themselves Students for Black Culture.

Seeks Improvement

Just as its motto implies, SBC aims for improvement in the relationship between races and between students and the faculty.

Another chief purpose of the organization is to provide its members, consisting of both black and white students, with an insight into the culture and history of the black man.

The organization is playing a major role in promoting National Negro History Week at Central. The Week will be observed at Central February 9-14.

Gains Publicity

SBC gained statewide publicity during the earlier part of the school year when, at one of its meetings, plans were made to walk out of classes to protest alleged grievances that black students had against the school.

The walkout involved approximately 100 students, all of whom were suspended from classes.

"Contrary to what some people may believe," said Robert Griffin, chairman of the organization, "SBC does not serve as an adversary of the administra-

PROMOTION—Sketching posters encouraging students to join Students for Black Culture during the club's second semester drive are (from left) Lillie Ingram, Rosemary Freeman, Larry Harrison, and Elaine Goolsby.

tion; in fact, we try to work with school administrators in a coordinated effort to encourage racial harmony."

Membership Open

Membership in the organization is open to any student who has an interest in learning more about black culture and in promoting racial harmony.

Dues are $1 per semester.

The dues may be paid to Griffin or Earthine Jones, secretary of the organization.

Sam Young, instructor of industrial arts, is faculty sponsor.

Meetings of the organization are every other Tuesday night at 7:30. The meetings are usually conducted at Campus Inn.

Integration Starts In September '57

Central integrated its classes on September 25, 1957, when nine black students were enrolled on their third attempt to end segregation in the school.

Their enrollment, ordered by a federal court, created a crisis within the city that gained worldwide publicity.

The school's faculty was integrated in September of 1965 with the arrival of Mrs. Opal Harper, who remains as an instructor of English.

In every issue, an issue. The Little Rock Central High Tiger *is known particularly for its reporting in depth. In this issue of January 30, 1970, the nation's Blacks are the subject. Five stories about five separate phases of the topic. Artwork to help brighten the page. Here, an issue is explored by several articles. Other issues might be explored by one long article.*

every society there are persons symbolically who burn down Reichstags (as did Adolf Hitler) and who then use the methods of mass communication (as did Hitler) to accuse their opponents of the misdeed (as did Hitler the communists and the Jews). Superficial reporting gives countenance and credibility to those propaganda proclamations. Those are "facts"—that a national leader did make such claims. But truth goes much further; the reporter must try to dig deeper than the level of Fact to find out if Truth be there buried.

To quote an authority in communications, Professor George N. Gordon: "So forceful is the desire of the human organism to make sense of his environment, that he will usually rush to the first ostensibly meaningful construction of his perceptions. . . . The *real* issues are avoided because bogus cognitive issues are too satisfying." [1]

Politicians and advertisers who depend upon public support realize the importance of (1) fragmented information, which can lead to favorable misperception, (2) first impressions, and (3) absence of counter-ideas. Thus, Vice-President Spiro T. Agnew in 1969 attacked the analysis by commentators that usually followed a speech by the President. Agnew's argument: The President's words should not be subjected to what he called "instant analysis," even though by experts. Agnew successfully eliminated any further post-speech analysis and therefore scored the propaganda victory of the decade. Television gave the President a chance to present (1) fragmented information—only that favorable to his position, to make a powerful (2) first impression— as only TV can provide, and to allow his arguments (3) to stand unopposed.

Post-speech analysis had been a matter of in-depth reporting— a first step to viewing a significant public political event in all its factual veracity, ideas, and backgrounding. The "Why" could be searched for!

---

[1] *The Language of Communication,* Hastings House, 1969, p. 172.

Rudyard Kipling wrote in 1902 in his still-popular *Just-So Stories* (in "The Elephant's Child");

> I keep six honest serving-men
> (They taught me all I knew);
> Their names are What and Why and When
> And How and Where and Who.

The most honest of the serving men, who have taught most of what man should know, are not necessarily When and Where and What and Who, but more important HOW and WHY.

To Do, to Read, to Think About

1. Study the depth stories in one week's issue of *The Wall Street Journal*—for subject matter, for obvious techniques of reporting and writing, for the level of their appeal to readers.

2. In a pocket notebook, begin to compile a list of "simplisms" as you hear them and read them. Note the sources. They can be used for class or staff comparisons and discussions. The next point—on what ignorance, emotion, self-delusion, or self-satisfaction are those simplisms constructed? Do the same for a list of symbols to which people react emotionally—such as long hair, the peace symbol, race.

3. Study announcements from government officials. Try to identify purposeful fragmentation of information. What specific questions are unanswered that must be answered if Truth is to be arrived at?

4. Put advertising messages, slogans, claims, and jingles to the test of (1) what isn't said, (2) what needs to be answered and is not, and (3) what is obviously exaggerated out of proportion. Then ask yourself whether advertising and political propaganda may not be two ways of man's establishing improper priorities.

5. What to read: *Persuasion,* by Sister Ann Christine Heintz.

(Loyola University Press, 1970.) A workbook-textbook designed to sharpen awareness of manipulation of public opinion and personal attitudes.

Books and articles about propaganda and public opinion.

An American Melodrama, by Lewis Chester, Godfrey Hodgson, Bruce Page. (The Viking Press, 1969.) The best account of the heavily manipulated political campaign of 1968. Also: *The Selling of the President,* by Joe McGinniss.

For accounts of the incomplete reporting in the early years of the war in Vietnam—the book *The Making of a Quagmire,* by David Halberstam, and the book *The New Face of War,* by Malcolm Browne.

For details about reporting see chapters in *The Student Journalist and Common News Assignments,* by Bill Ward. (Richards Rosen Press, 1971.) Also *Newspapering,* by Bill Ward. (National Scholastic Press Association, revised 1971.)

6. For a current controversy in your school, outline the vital questions to be answered (the Why's), list all persons who must be interviewed to get a complete report of the problem, list all documents and records that should be researched, examine the history of the controversy and try to project the possible future results of it. This would be the beginning of a plan for reporting a story in depth. Follows Points 1–9 listed on pages 34–35.

7. For a "first-time" story in a newspaper—the first report of a story—study it carefully for incomplete information, for possible misinformation, for the questions not answered, for possible transmission of propaganda. Then follow stories in successive days to note finally any serious deviations between "Truth" in the first and the final news reports.

FIVE DEPTH STORY IDEAS

1. How true is it that students today do not read as much as students of past generations, that they form a "visual" generation turned off from newspapers, books, and magazines?

2. What does "long hair" for young males symbolize to the wearers and to the beholders—the suggestion frequently repeated that long hair is the most controversial symbol of our times?

3. What does the slogan "America: love it or leave it" really mean and symbolize to the various members of the student generation?

4. What else can (and do) tests during courses accomplish other than measuring the extent of a student's fund of information?

5. What is the story behind the architecture of your school, of your campus?

A Course in Dullness for Reporters?

Student editors and reporters who are intent on raising the level of their stories and are directing themselves more toward depth reporting, backgrounding the news, and news features have an ally in Stuart A. Dunham who, as editor of the Camden, New Jersey, *Courier-Post,* made the following appeal for more relevant news. The appeal appeared in *The Gannetteer,* official magazine for Gannett Newspapers, in January, 1966.

What I found, and still find, is a local news coverage that is a vast gray monotony, broken only occasionally by a spark of interest.

I find that city hall news about important subjects is mostly written in the terms of procedure and in the language of city ordinances.

I find that police news is written like a formal entry in the police blotter.

I find plenty of stories about turkey night at the K of C and the dedication of a new school, complete with formal set speeches.

I find story after story about highway accidents, but never a story of what it is really like at the scene of just one accident.

Gambling arrests are duly reported, but never a glimpse into the life of one gambler or the $2 bettor whose money supports the machine.

There is the feature story about the farmer who raises extraordinarily large pumpkins, but never a real glimpse into the daily routine of the farmer as he starts for his barn in the hours before dawn.

There are plenty of stories about the next tour of the high school glee club, but never a real look at the daily life of a teacher or her pupils.

The turnpike threads like an artery through a mobile society. Occasionally I find a story about a diplomat being ushered off the turnpike, but never a story about the plight of the stranded motorist or an evaluation of today's driver by a turnpike policeman.

There are sociological speeches and statistics about alcoholism, but nothing from the bartender who may have watched a successful businessman slide into the gutter.

Women's pages are great for listing the chairmen for the next garden-club meetings, but if there is any frustration or loneliness among housewives, it will be reported only in Dear Abby.

In short, a tour through the local news coverage of the dailies is too often a trip through Dullsville. I know from experience that these cities and towns are interesting places, just as interesting as James Joyce's Dublin, or William Faulkner's Oxford, Miss.

True, many daily newspapers are limited in their resources. In-depth studies have to be selected carefully because of the skill and time involved. But does this mean that the daily coverage has to read like a proxy statement?

I know of one young man who had been a reporter for only a month or so. He covered a fatal accident which occurred just outside his newspaper office. He wrote an adequate story against deadline. A day or so later he went over his notes and his recollections, and wrote a short piece on just what was said and done at the scene of the accident. It proved to me that even a cub reporter can write a simple, unadorned but very compelling account of an accident.

We have the manpower. A stenographer with a tape recorder in a saloon could come up with more interesting local copy than I read in the dailies, and not just more interesting but more pertinent to the way people live and think.

I don't think it is difficult for newspapers to get into the main-stream of life. What puzzles me is how they so often manage to stay out of it.

#

"As I see it, interpretation—or background (I make no difference) —is the deeper sense of the news. It gives meaning to the bare facts; it places an event in the larger flow of events. It is in short, setting, sequence, and, above all, significance."

—Lester Markel
Sunday editor, New York Times.

FEWER ROUTINE NEWS ITEMS. More in-depth reporting of important news. That is the philosophy of the staff of The U-High Midway *(University High School, Chicago, Illinois). Here, the entire front page is devoted to reporting in depth a new educational program—mostly by "packaged" reporting. One story to the report, in general. One story about reactions from teachers and students. One story to reprinting important segments of the report. Magazine layout. Overprinting on a gray screen. The page is dynamic in appearance.*

Chapter III

SUBJECTS AND TOPICS FOR IN-DEPTH REPORTING

Almost anything could become the topic for reporting in depth. Look, for instance, at the range of topics used during one brief period by *The Wall Street Journal*.

But before deciding to go ahead with an idea, you should put it to the following tests.

1. *Is there need for the eventual story—or is there strong local interest?* To launch an investigation of tax-free properties in the community may be wasted effort—like firing ammunition at the sky—if when all is reported the reader says: "So what?!" There are tax-free properties, but no one has made an issue of them, no one is contemplating a change in their status, in tax dollars they don't amount to much, the only news value would be for "knowing" or in some featurized approach. And just because one newspaper wins a Pulitzer Prize for an investigation in its community into corruption involving such tax loopholes does not mean the same situation exists in your community. Illegal abortion is a problem at one college, but certainly not at another. A change from the quarter system to the semester system may be in-depth material at one school; at another it may never have been mentioned.

2. *Is your topic specific enough?* It must be narrowly defined before you start the reporting, not when you sit down to write the story. You would not attempt to report in depth this topic:

Changes in teaching—such as modular scheduling

You want a more specific topic line to investigate, posed perhaps in these words:

How will modular scheduling affect students in this school when it is introduced next year?

You know exactly where you are going. You have a point in the distance on which to focus all your questions and your information. You are sure the topic is limited enough to be handled in a reasonable period of time in a limited amount of space. You are sure it is planned to be of direct interest to the readers. You are not interested in modular scheduling as a theory of education; you want to know *how it touches the students—your readers —personally.*

The weak general topic	*The better specific topic-line*
ROTC on campus	What are the probabilities of the present ROTC program on campus being turned over to a regional ROTC center?
Writing among students	In this age of television and film, do students show talent at and interest in writing prose and poetry?
Computerized school records	Is computerization on campus increasing efficiency at the cost of depersonalizing the students?
State athletic tournaments	Do major sports events "professionalize" school sports; and are they in accordance with the purposes for interscholastic sports?
Pressures and tensions on students	To what degree do the pressures of going to school cause serious psychological, emotional, and other problems among students?

You will note that most questions can be answered specifically: yes, my reporting shows it is probable the regional ROTC program will be established within five years! That is the timely, relevant, and interesting discovery you would transmit to the reader. Your story will report all the information you have gathered pertinent to that conclusion. Even disproof of your hypothesis makes a story: "No, all evidence indicates sports are not being unduly professionalized." You became interested in the story because debate had developed over the topic. Your refutation of the charge makes an equally good story.

Sometimes, your findings will be less decisive. "No, computerization is not proving more efficient, and, yes, it is depersonalizing students." The information behind those conclusions—well, there is the story in depth.

3. *Is the topic timely?* A study of enrollment growth is more pertinent at enrollment time—early fall or late spring—than it would be, say, at Christmas time: A study of increasing costs of education is timely when a bond issue or a tax hike is being publicly discussed. Certainly, a depth report about snow tires is of interest at the start of winter; it is of little interest in midsummer. There must be a reason for the story's being reported and written *now*, rather than next month or several issues ago.

4. *Do you have reasonable access to the necessary information?* An in-depth study of teenage girl delinquents would be impractical if you could not consult with state and national experts, too, or could not visit detention homes, or could not get names of girls to interview. You would have only an interview story with a local juvenile officer—and that single step in reporting does not make a depth story.

5. *Is there really "depth" to your story idea?* Just because a Campus Christian Association has been formed does not mean you have an idea for a depth story. The new organization would provide a news story. But no depth story—unless the new association can be coupled with other evidence to suggest a trend in the attitudes of students toward religion. "Is there a revolutionary

trend among students in their attitudes toward formalized religion?" This topic-line may be suggested most recently by the new association; that at least is where you would start your reporting.

Or the topic of men's hairstyling would make a good, one-time feature if some barber is doing something new and unusual. Hairstyles would become a possibility for in-depth reporting only if you could do something much more complex to it—such as this topic-line:

To students does their long hair symbolize a new life-style of their own or does it indicate mostly a rejection of the "old world" and its life-style?

Why do students let hair grow long? In the "Why" there is depth! In the Who (Charlie Bernardi, the Barber) doing What (trying to advocate the Mohawk cut), there is only a feature story.

6. *Has your topic been explained too many times?* The worst possible fault of a depth story—it is an echo! Readers sense they have seen the material before. And they may have—in a magazine on a national basis, in last year's newspaper, during a television documentary. You have explored no new ground. You have merely repeated what a person already knows, or supports. For a time, it was fashionable to report abortions. Then it was sex education. Then it was dress codes. Then it was environmental pollution, and the Greek System (is it declining in power?), and parking problems. Those topics—all important enough—began to suffer from overexposure. Only when a new and vital topic-line is developed can triteness be avoided.

Does enforcement of parking regulations seriously impair execution of the other responsibilities and duties of security police on campus?
Are community politics linked in any way with pro- and anti-sex education movements?

How is the average student on this campus directly and specifically affected by environmental pollution?

Expressing Unpopular Opinions—Definitely Unpopular

The least understood of valued rights among school-age youngsters and young adults is *the freedom to express controversial or unpopular opinions.* A survey in 1970 about "citizenship" showed that startling result. The findings were released by the federally supported National Assessment of Educational Progress (NAEP).

Confronted by three controversial statements about religion, politics, and race and asked whether those topics should be allowed on radio or television, students answered this way:

> 13-year-olds—94 percent NO.
> 17-year-olds—78 percent NO.
> Young adults—68 percent NO.

In another part of the survey, 54 percent of the 17-year-olds said they thought they could personally influence government—despite the fact they did not strongly endorse television discussion of controversial statements. But only 11 percent could enumerate several ways to affect government.

Overall the results predict considerable difficulty for depth reportage in student newspapers about such highly emotional topics as "race." It seems that a majority of students were admitting that they felt—along with a majority of school administrators—that some topics are better forgotten, or debate left unscheduled.

---

7. *Is your topic-line down to earth; is it close to the interest-level of most of your readers?* Your student readers in general are not much interested in micro-teaching as a new method being used in the schools of education for preparing teachers. But they may be interested in how micro-teaching will improve the

performance of the new, young teachers they will be studying under in the next year or two. The possible topic-line: "How will micro-teaching put a better teacher in the classroom in the next year or two?"

8. *Is the topic-line negative or too sensational, leading you to a dishonest conclusion?* "What is wrong with ROTC?" You obviously have slanted the story. Better: "Why have 25 percent of freshman ROTC students dropped from the corps since the start of the year?"

9. *Does your topic lend itself to illustrations, to photographs, cartoons, or other artwork?* You would not discard an idea if the answer here is "No." But the long text of a depth story needs to be displayed brightly, and you must plan eventually for a lookable story as well as a readable one.

10. *Have you examined your topic-line one more time to be sure it is clear, specific, honest—and workable?* Once underway, you should not alter seriously the topic-line. Any one topic can lead to a book if you report assertively enough.

When submitting your suggestions for depth stories to an editor, first type the topic-line. Then outline as fully as possible ideas for reporting the story, your thinking about its importance and interest, and some of what you know already about it. Editors when assigning ideas should provide the same outline for reporters.

Students of journalism asked to submit ideas for depth stories have made these fundamental missteps:

Idea	*Fault*
1. Auxiliary enterprises.	1. ??? Meaningless???
2. How much is stolen from the school each year?	2. Poor topic-line leads to facts-only news story, not story in depth.
3. The "modern" fraternity.	3. What about it???

4. Do members of the board (of education, or of trustees) have the qualifications necessary for their job?

4. Good idea—but is it timely enough?

5. Is credit good or bad for people?

5. Too general a topic-line—and too polarized.

6. Backstage on opening night.

6. Not depth story—it is a sights and sounds feature.

7. The new rise in tuition.

7. A news story unless you construct a topic-line for it, such as, "Will the rise in tuition cause students to drop out of the school?"

8. Voting at 18.

8. Too general—how about: How will students in this school vote next year when allowed to at age 18.

Back full circle to the opening words of this chapter. Almost anything can become the topic for reporting in depth—as long as you can see into the topic sufficiently to construct a strong topic-line.

Don't set out on a trip into unfamiliar country unless you have a satisfactory map.

Don't presume to undertake depth reporting unless you have before you a satisfactory topic-line.

To Do, to Read, to Think About

1. From a list of general topics (such as "new fads and fashions"), construct a set of topic-lines that could lead to depth stories. From several persons should come several varying topic-lines about the same subject.

Just supposing . . .

Ins and outs are replacing goods and bads. There is a shift from the old norms, the linear patterns, to a new, continuous, simultaneous way of life. Rigid forms are giving way to flexible patterns. McLuhan is a prophet, not a propagator, of these changes. Who knows? maybe some day . . .

OUTS	INS
printed books	taped books
logic	intuition
scooter relays	maul ball
It's Academic	personal computer boxes
line-up	huddle
drinking	games
appointments	chance meetings
scripts	improvisations
I	we
chorus lines	circle two-step
square houses	round houses
childhood	?

Sound of the times

Many of Marshall McLuhan's theories can be substantiated by the popular music of today.

Music matches our electronically-oriented society in that the music and lyrics are thrown at the listener at the same time; yet there is a basic driving force to it — the beat. The effect of this is to present a pulsating rhythm without any one group member guiding the performance.

Too often, critics of the modern music young people want, say that that the listeners can't possibly understand the meaning of the various songs because everything is grouped together into a single wall of sound.

Only a few years ago, these critics point out, the singer was the main performer with the band complementing his efforts. Now, the listener receives an electronic barrage with the singer in direct competition with the other band members.

The strange thing about everything played together in a compact, driving rhythm is that the listeners can perceive what is happening. It is no longer necessary for the listeners to hear the singer as such because they understand, or sense the meaning, without distinctly hearing the lyrics.

This substantiates McLuhan's theory that the electronically-oriented young have the ability to grasp everything at once.

In music, our society may have accepted a tribal influence. That is, an influence where the individual's reactions are fundamental to the controlling force.

A point of evidence in favor of McLuhan's theories is that listeners must react in some way to modern music.

Every listener complies with the driving force and reacts in a fundamental manner, usually dancing with no set pattern to follow, combining action with immediate reaction.

The theories of Marshall McLuhan aren't far off; they're visible in our world today.

You can go back to the game now!

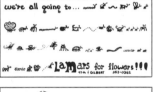

Standing on the corner, waiting

Chicago, or any big city, is a parade of society. It contains so many people that almost every aspect of modern culture is represented. In a big city, if anywhere, the observations of Marshall McLuhan are confirmed or disproved.

In *Division Street America*, journalist, social commentator, and interviewer Studs Terkel has attempted to distill the city's problems into a single volume.

ARMED WITH TAPE recorder and a talent for coaxing the thoughts from people's minds, Terkel has amassed some seventy self-portraits that show the character of the city and of modern living.

Terkel's subjects speak from all walks of life. All colors and creeds spill out their impressions on everything from suburban living to "The Bomb." Their language is accurately reproduced complete with colloquialisms, glibness, sarcasm, or sorrow and the result is a rare and refreshingly vital book.

PERHAPS TERKEL himself describes it best. "This book is in no way intended as a survey. Nor is it an attempt to spell out conclusions, joyful or joyless, about Chicago. It is neither the believer's Good News nor the doubter's bad report.

Once over lightly

"Electrical technology" has perpetrated a revolution in the human environment, according to McLuhan in *The Medium is the Massage*.

The nature of this revolution — a "reshaping and restructuring" of "patterns of social interdependence" — is universal change, an upheaval in every aspect of our environment.

McLUHAN EMPHASIZES this, that everything is changing — you, your family, neighborhood, education, job, government, and relation to others.

Society is shaped more by the nature of its media than by content, which explains how, with a total integration of electronic media, such a vast change can occur.

Individuals are probably most radically affected by the electronic revolution.

INDIVIDUAL THOUGHT and action is threatened by the circuitry take-over, whose "universal, tyrannical womb-to-tomb surveillance" brings the right to privacy and the community's growing necessity for information into conflict. In this McLuhan world, everyone is involved.

Neighborhoods are no longer tightly-knit social groups — they are the entire area a single electronic system can dominate.

Earth has truly become a world community, says McLuhan. Individuals, neighborhoods, and the public have merged and blended to become the "mass audience." And the new environment compells his involvement, its participation.

With circuitry, people have become structured into their mass-media society. The separation of thought and action which existed in the "linear" or "sequential" environment of the type-written word has disappeared, making he world, as McLuhan states, once again "a village."

The LANGAS toe was reproduced with the permission of Sandy Smith '67.

"I WAS ON THE PROWL for a cross-section of urban thought, using no one method or technique. It was the man of inchoate thought I was seeking rather than the consciously articulate.

"Each of the subjects may have come to his belief or lack of it in his own ornery way; yet evidence seems overwhelming that mass media, with their daily litany of tribute to things rather than men, played their wondrous role.

"What have we here? There is a vague, uneasy — and in some fewer instances, exhilarating — awareness of events. There is no Before and After."

In the beginning —

The roots of this supplement sprang from the March 16 north campus assembly. Several staff members were considering an editorial on the poor student response, and two of them happened on McLuhan's "hot" and "cool" media. Hurriedly they procured copies of McLuhan's books and, as they found more and more examples of McLuhanism in the school, the idea for this special supplement arose. During the weeks between then and now, an estimated 300 man hours have gone into its production.

A bibliography of our McLuhan material is available, free for the asking, in the Lion office (105 N.C.)

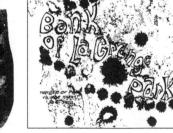

THE INSIDE PAGES OF THE SPECIAL McLUHAN ISSUE OF THE LION.

2. For one general, most important topic (student power in the school), construct several topic-lines that could be used by several reporters, the several depth stories to be packaged into a special supplement or magazine.

3. For possible topic-lines look at the areas of student culture, too—not just politics and education. For possible ideas, examine the key words and phrases of:

FAITH	SECURITY	CONSUMER OF BOOKS
CHANGE	POPULAR CULTURE	EASIER, HAPPIER LIFE
HEALTH	PROGRESS	SELF-ADVANCEMENT

4. Study depth stories in *The Wall Street Journal, The National Observer, The Christian Science Monitor,* etc. for those that could be adapted to your campus, for publication in the school newspaper or magazine.

5. What problems most affect your readers? Here are sources for depth stories. What are your readers really concerned about? And remember, don't expect readers to think as you do! What problems are distinctive to your campus, your students, your community? Here are the sources of your best depth ideas.

6. Read education magazines for ideas: *Saturday Review* education section, *The New York Times* Sunday education section, *Change, NEA Journal, The Chronicle of Higher Education.*

7. Journalists tend to become overly skeptical and they must balance themselves by consciously seeking "good news." Develop two topic-lines with accompanying descriptions for stories that could be called "positive."

FIVE DEPTH STORY IDEAS

1. Does school life affect negatively in any way a student's health, manners, security, faith, or morality? How about the balance sheet between positive and negative effects?

2. This is an age of self-publishing, by mimeograph, by un-

derground press, etc. How strong is the will for such self-expression and communication on your campus?

3. How extensively does popular culture become part of what is taught in the curriculum of your school—whether acid rock in music or "found poetry" or use of acrylics and other modern media in art?

4. How far ahead of the times is your school, in part or whole?

5. Student credit (cards, charge accounts, etc.)—of one form or another: How important has it become to the financial life of students?

Chapter IV

THE RESEARCH

You are reporting and writing for the Press; you are not preparing a term paper. Therefore, most of your information must be gotten from observations and interviews, by on-the-spot and firsthand techniques. You rely mostly on *primary information*—what you, yourself, gather and put together into a particular form for the first time.

Unfortunately, most students have been trained by the "term paper" to merely collate *secondary information*—in fact, to plagiarize outrightly the firsthand work of other persons. "If you steal from one person," Wilson Mizner, a wit, once said, "it is plagiarism. If you steal from many it's research." Well, substitute "term paper" for "research." The effect of the term paper has been disastrous on both the research methods and the thinking processes of students. Select a topic; go to several reference books and collect data (too often in the exact prose of those writers), and then somehow string those extracts into a paper that is badly disjointed from the bits and pieces of borrowing. The task has been turned over to teachers of English, sadly enough because the term paper is neither literature nor good writing. Yet senior-level courses in English are dedicated to the proposition of the term paper ("to get you ready for college"), and freshman composition in college is dedicated to the proposition of the term paper ("to get you ready for the upper-class challenge of college"), and somewhere along the line the student learns not to think but to imitate, not to write but to transcribe, not to research but to extract, not to be independent but to be thoroughly reliant.

58

The saddest of all about term papers—it becomes an accumulative process without the student's even bothering to challenge the logic and evidence of his sources. A graduate student in college devised a system for all term papers: a set number of sources referred to, a set number of bibliographical entries whether used or not, a set number of pages to the report, and a set number of footnotes, of extracts. He could do a term paper in an afternoon, he boasted of it, and he never got below a B. "Even if it is a boring paper," he said, "I have measured up to all the mechanical expectations, and that is worth a B. When the teacher doesn't bother to read it, the mechanical perfection gets me an A."

So much for the term paper, which to the journalist's mind is misguided work. He is more interested in a well-defined topic of special interest and moment to readers. He is intent on digging out his own information, firsthand, put together in an original manner. To write about juvenile delinquency among teenage girls, he will talk to officers, probation people, delinquents themselves, parents, etc., etc., etc. He will visit juvenile halls and the school of correction. He may follow one case from arrest to arrival at the school of correction. From this mass of *primary* information, never before collected into an article or report, he will write a story in depth. Thus, he shuns the weak-minded principles of the "term paper."

Yet the depth reporter will use, to an extent, research among printed materials. But his is not an automatic dash to the encyclopedia to compendiously copy it into a report. His research is not limited to a check of the almanac or a collection of pilferages from books that are the result of someone else's laborious *primary* research. The reporter looks among printed materials for these points:

(1) Authoritative facts from reputable sources to add to his information. He will accredit such sources within his article, not in footnotes.

(2) Knowledge of what already has been written and pub-

ORBIT

Volume 8—No. 6   John Overton High School — Nashville, Tennessee   February 19, 1970

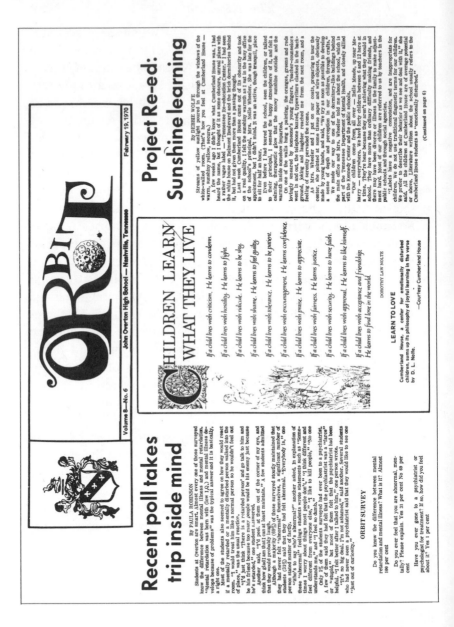

Recent poll takes trip inside mind

By PAULA ROBINSON

Students at Overton are smart. Almost every one of those surveyed know the difference between mental retardation and mental illness. "Mental retardation was born with (low I.Q.) and mental illness develops because of problems" was the typical answer and it is basically a right one.

Most of the students also seemed to agree on how they would react if a mentally retarded or a mentally disturbed person walked into the room. "I would trust him like a normal person so he wouldn't feel out of place," was the usual reaction.

"I'd just think 'there is a retarded person' and go talk to him and be his friend because too many people would be his enemy just because he's retarded," one student answered.

Another said, "I'd run out of the corner of my eye, and think how glad I am that I can at least maintain." A few students admitted that they would probably laugh.

Although a majority (69%) of those surveyed study maintained that they had never felt "abnormal" themselves, a significant number of students (31%) said that they had felt abnormal. "Everybody is," one person stated matter of factly.

"Who's to say who's abnormal?" another asked. In explanation of these "abnormal" feelings students wrote statements such as "Sometimes I worry about things most people don't," "I think different and feel different from everyone else," "I like to kill people," "No one understands me," and "I feel so dumb."

A few of them said they had felt that the psychiatrist was a "nurse" or "stupid," but most of them felt that the psychiatrist had been helpful. "I felt better after I talked to him," one person wrote.

"It's no big deal. I'm not ashamed," said another. Several students who had never seen a psychiatrist said that they would like to see one "just out of curiosity."

ORBIT SURVEY

Do you know the difference between mental retardation and mental illness? What is it? Almost 100 per cent

Do you ever feel that you are abnormal, mentally? Please explain. Yes 31 per cent No 69 per cent

Have you ever gone to a psychiatrist or psychologist for treatment? If so, how did you feel about it? Yes 1 per cent

CHILDREN LEARN WHAT THEY LIVE

If a child lives with criticism, He learns to condemn.

If a child lives with hostility, He learns to fight.

If a child lives with ridicule, He learns to be shy.

If a child lives with shame, He learns to feel guilty.

If a child lives with tolerance, He learns to be patient.

If a child lives with encouragement, He learns confidence.

If a child lives with praise, He learns to appreciate.

If a child lives with fairness, He learns justice.

If a child lives with security, He learns to have faith.

If a child lives with approval, He learns to like himself.

If a child lives with acceptance and friendship, He learns to find love in the world.

DOROTHY LAW NOLTE

LEARN TO LOVE

Cumberland House, a center for emotionally disturbed children, sums up its philosophy of joyful learning in the verse above.

—Courtesy Cumberland House

Project Re-ed: Sunshine learning

By DEBBIE WOLFE

Streams of yellow sunlight poured in through the windows of the white-walled room. (That's how you feel at Cumberland House — warm, sunshiny yellow, secure.)

A few weeks ago I didn't know what Cumberland House was. I had heard the name, but I thought of it as some obscure, unreal place with a rather vague label — "Tennessee re-education Center." I had seen the white house on Belmont Boulevard and the brick dormitories behind it, but had not given them more than a passing thought.

Last week Cumberland House came out of its obscurity and took on a real quality. I felt the sunshiny warmth as I sat in the busy office of the school's principal, Mrs. Nelle Wheeler. She was late for the appointment, but I didn't mind. It was an active, though tranquil, place to sit for half an hour.

Even before I had toured the school, seen the children, or talked to their principal, I sensed the happy atmosphere of it, and felt a calming, therapeutic glow that the snowy sunshine outside and the warmth inside somehow imparted.

On one of the walls hung a painting, the oranges, greens and reds lovingly smeared by someone's young fingers. Teacher-counselors went in and out, the telephone buzzed, typewriters clacked in the background, joking and laughter reached me from the next room, and a feeling of serenity pervaded the scene.

As Mrs. Wheeler and I put on our coats, preparing to tour the center, she pointed at some tissue paper and wire objects, obviously made by young hands, and said, "We try as soon as possible to develop a sense of depth and perception in our children, through crafts."

We made our way to one of the dormitory-like buildings behind the main office and Mrs. Wheeler told me about the school, which is part of the Tennessee Department of Mental Health, and closely allied with the Kennedy Center and the public schools.

"Our children come from all over — Belle Meade, up near Metro-Center — everywhere. We hard forty children between 6 and 12 here at a time. They're here because they aren't achieving what they should in school. They have more than ordinary difficulty making friends, and there may have been divorce or illness in the family to make adjustment hard. Most of our children are referred to us by teachers in the public schools and through social agencies.

"Labels have a negative connotation, and are inappropriate for children. We do not use traditional diagnostic terms for our children. We prefer to describe their behavior as we see and deal with it," she said. All the children at Cumberland House are of average potential or above. Literature written about the school usually refers to the Cumberland House students as "emotionally disturbed."

(Continued on page 6)

lished about the topic so he can at least find a new angle or point of view for a fresh approach.

(3) An idea of the arguments and opinions about the topic so he can more intelligently interview his sources and understand the comments about prevailing points of view. He needs general background information from which to report.

(4) The history, perhaps, of the subject, which might be blended into his final story.

(5) Definitions and explanations of terms and functions he will be working with.

(6) Leads in directories to organizations and persons who can supply him with further information.

(7) Factual information (biographical) about persons and institutions he will be interviewing and observing. With such basic information in hand he will be able to devote reporting time to more complex questions.

EXPERIMENT!—sometimes success, sometimes not. To find new patterns to reporting, writing, and displaying the news, the young staff of the Orbit *swung heavily to what commercially had been called The New Journalism. Personalized reporting, essay style and structure for stories, stress on in-depth reporting, dynamic new page 1's All come together on this page 1, about mental retardation and education. A personalized, first-hand observations story—written in dramatic narrative—began in column 3. In column 1, a poll among students about their knowledge of such special education. In the center column, the credo of a house for emotionally disturbed children. The entire page 1 was set sideways rather than in the usual vertical format to create this unusual appearance for a brilliantly executed piece of work.*

A great many enthusiasts for the student press were disappointed in 1970 when the Orbit *(John Overton High School, Nashville) was not named a Pacemaker (one of five best in the country). It had gone where other staffs had not envisioned going. It proved students can write powerfully, that newspapers can be much more loose in physical appearance, that students must care about the world outside the classroom. Under its young adviser, Martha Jean Greenfield, it set a pattern not soon to be forgotten.*

(8) Sometimes, in print research he will find most of his information—but always in documents, records, deeds, and so on, which is noncollated, primary material.

Surprisingly, most writers of term papers never get into their topics as extensively. And at best the research ends at the library exit.

The depth reporter, however, is just getting started—the first stage only completed.

For general background to the subject, the reporter may have time for extensive research in *secondary* materials. Magazine articles, newspaper clip files, books, and pamphlets. But he does *not* note heavily. He is after general background, a feeling for the topic. If he does note a few points, it is for follow-up during later interviews. If he does note facts, he must later double-check their accuracy and be sure, if used, he knows to whom to accredit them. He goes mostly to these sources:

Reader's Guide to Periodical Literature—A listing of magazine articles according to topic. There are several such series of books, special volumes for science, for education, even for literary magazines and for book reviews. Here the reporter gets general background information as well as an idea of what new angles to follow and what old topics have been explored.

Current Biography—Facts about significant contemporary persons. There are also several biographical dictionaries, and a great many volumes of biography especially for scholars (*Directory of American Scholars*) and authors (*American Authors and Books*) and *Who's Who* editions according to profession and geography (*Who's Who in the Midwest*). There is also an historical *Who Was Who in America,* treating 13,350 subjects.

Webster's Geographical (or *Biographical*) *Dictionary*—Here the reporter double-checks spellings—and perhaps gets a more specific idea of locations so he can refer more clearly to their whereabouts. In depth reporting all such factual information must be scrupulously checked. Also helpful: the *U.S. Postal Guide,* and city directories.

Statistical Abstract of the United States—A wealth of facts past and present, which may add to the story. There are thousands of such statistical compilations—every state government publishes at least one, as well as legislative manuals, yearbooks, and compilations of legislation passed and proposed. And county and city governments. And federal and state agencies. And corporations (in their annual reports). And special commissions. Libraries abound in such statistical information that may enhance a depth story. (Yet facts are only secondary in interest to human interest in news.) General almanacs, such as the *World Almanac,* will sometimes provide worthwhile details. Special almanacs, too, such as *The Economic Almanac.*

New York Times Index—Each daily issue of that newspaper is annotated by topic, and if a reporter wants to track down news stories about recent events and situations (this is considered primary information), he can find days of issues and page numbers and refer on microfilm to the *Times.* Or using the day a story appears in the *Times,* he might trace a similar story on that same day in another daily newspaper. *The Wall Street Journal,* too, has an index. *Facts on File,* too, provides a daily account of the news. A great many Books of the Year summarize each year in news, or in business, or in agriculture, and so on. *The Congressional Record* (a primary resource) reports for each day all the functions of Congress, a must for research. Also! *Congressional Quarterly.*

Encyclopedia of Social Sciences—When trying to track down an idea or a philosophy or a technique, the reporter can find basic explanations in such specialized sets of encyclopedias as this one. Others exist for physical science and for art. The reporter thus is pre-armed for intelligent questions in his interviews. Special dictionaries explain terms, too, such as *Black's Law Dictionary.*

To use library resources fully and properly, a reporter should spend an afternoon browsing through available libraries, noting carefully the materials he might effectively use. Every library is different, some inclusive, some infrequent in such basic reference materials.

No reference has been made here to general encyclopedias. They are too much collated and reduced in content to be of much functional value for the reporter.

The reporter must remember, however, that in the library he is *preparing* himself for the story. This work in the library is a first, preparatory step—not, as for the term paper, the full trip.

Some other ideas of reference books for various usages:

Books in Print—To trace publishers and availability of books. Also: *Book Review Digest,* a yearly collection of reviews

Card Catalog—To track down special books by author, or more valuably by topic, or by title. Book indexes provide fast reference, within a book, to special information.

Vertical files—For pamphlets that generally have more value to reporters than the generalized books.

Yearbook of American Churches or *Patterson's Educational Directory*—Helpful in finding addresses and names, in counting numbers of, say, schools in an area.

Guide to Reference Books or *Basic Reference Sources*—Several books are helpful in referring you to library resources you have never thought of.

Editorial Research Reports—Exhaustively reports backgrounds of contemporary problems, issues, and situations. These reports are used by editorial writers mostly, and are *copyrighted*.

The Encyclopedia of American Facts and Dates—Helpful in double-checking material. Excellent for ideas for historical features. *Famous First Facts. Encyclopedia of American History. The Rapid Fact Finder. Chase's Calendar of Events.*

Bartlett's Familiar Quotations—To track down lively quotes, by topics, which for one reason or another might blend into a story.

Encyclopedia of Associations—Excellent for finding, by topic too, special associations and organizations (as of laundromat operators) that may be able to supplement your information.

General encyclopedias. Be wary of them. Despite the 36,000,-000 words in the *Britannica,* or the 28,500,000 words in the *Americana,* or the 21,000,000 words in *Collier's,* the material is too much reduced and simplified and prospected over to be of much value to you. For instance, the single-volume *The Columbia Encyclopedia* consists of 7,500,000 words split among 75,000 articles.

Book of States—Much useful data about recent legislation.

The reporter must not bury himself in the library. That is not the source of most of the material he works with. In fact, some depth stories may never take him to the library. Or deadline pressures may reduce his preliminary research to absolute minimum. He will find himself going quite often to the library to check out material *while he is in the stage of reporting.*

As a researcher, the reporter will devote most of his time to original documents and files. Court records. Deeds on file. Minutes of past meetings and such official proceedings. All kinds of public records. Bids and the subsequent contracts awarded. Transcripts of court cases. Diaries and journals of individuals. Annual reports. Tax assessor's records. County auditor's reports. Writs and reports in the prosecutor's office. Police blotter. Reports from special commissions and transcripts of testimony from meetings of commissions. Mortgages on record. Bank statements. Expense accounts. *Here is the gold mine of depth reporting.* In all this original, unresearched, native material, the depth reporter finds rewarding information—generally unknown by the public and strongly reputable in his story.

For instance, the Billie Sol Estes exposé, which caused considerable discomfort to the administration of President Lyndon B. Johnson. A reporter for a small Texas newspaper was perplexed by the number of mortgages for sealed granaries he had seen filed in his county, each granary involved with federal subsidy. The reporter drove about the county counting granaries and comparing the filed documents with specific locations. He soon discovered discrepancy. A recurring name on the mortgages eventually led to Sol Estes.

The *Charlotte Observer* (North Carolina) won a Pulitzer Prize for exposing vote frauds that took reporters into documentary research with absentee ballots. For the *Riverside Press-Enterprise* (California), a reporter went into official court records to in part expose victimization through a "ward system" of Indians in the area. Community leaders in such proxy awards controlled property holdings on reservations. A state auditor in Illinois was found to have embezzled $2,500,000 only after a reporter had spent endless tedious hours checking through state financial records. No one else had done it; it took reporter George Thiem to do so. The *St. Petersburg Times* went into the records to prove that personal fortunes had been made by refinancing bonds of the state turnpike authority. A tip led to the investigation. A team of reporters and photographers worked on the story in depth. A total of 4,800 inches of space was devoted to stories, pictures, and editorials.

Whether you are writing a feature, news story, editorial, or story in depth, you as a reporter must be conscious of research into documents and records. You must know what is available, where it is, and then be eager to put days of tedious sorting—like George Thiem—into them. On rare occasions, here is most of your story. In most instances, here is at least part of your story. In no instance at all can you ignore research and documentation without in some way reducing the level and effectiveness of the story.

You as a reporter:

(1) research and document,

(2) participate and observe,

(3) interview,

to get the materials for a story. To report in depth you are willing to research, observe, and interview to the fullest—to mine far below the surface of things.

You are like one of the great reporters of all times, the American muckraker Lincoln Steffens. He investigated for most of a lifetime corruption in city government (read *Shame of the Cities*). It is doubtful if any reporter in history has risen higher than Steffens. (Or as opponents would say, "mucked lower.") He saw journalism as having to be heavily interpretive. He said that what a journalist needs most of all is, in his words, "not so much honesty as integrity." He described his significant reporting techniques as these:.

✔ **First of all, get on the scene.**

✔ **Give those persons being interviewed the idea he (Steffens) wanted to know them and all about their ideas.**

✔ **Observe keenly.**

✔ **And finally, as closing advice to the reporter in depth, <u>know</u> public records.**

To Do, to Read, to Think About

1. Go to a set of public records for your school—budgets over the years, minutes of meetings, series of continuing reports over the years (as from the principal administrator), tuition reports and per-student costs, textbook accounts, health reports—and put together at least one story for publication. That will give you practice working patiently with research materials, as well as teaching you to analyze and synthesize them!

2. Do the same with a recent public report—as might come from a special commission, or the city, or a taxpayers' task force. Or compare and contrast similar reports from various groups or from various years (as school budgets).

3. For familiarizing yourself with clipping files, write a biographical report about a person who has been prominent in the news. Or write an article for a column to be called: "(This school) Ten Years Ago." That will take you into old publications, and perhaps into old records and files.

4. Ask yourself questions that will take you into accumulated files and records, probably for feature stories and not so much depth stories:

What movie has drawn best attendance locally in recent years?

What items sell best in student book stores?

How much more has it cost over the years to educate each individual student?

Is June really the month of more marriages?

5. If you are interested in the career of Lincoln Steffens, read his *Autobiography,* especially the second half, which is concerned solely with his years as an investigative reporter.

6. For accounts of investigative stories, read John Hohenberg's collection of *Pulitzer Prize Winning Stories,* or his *The New Front Pages.*

7. Form a team to turn the local libraries inside out to compile a master list for all campus reporters, providing detailed information about what resource materials are available to fulfill what specific needs.

8. Using *The New York Times Index* or *Facts on File,* track down the recent history of a significant news event still being reported and use the information for a piece to be called "The (whatever the story) at a Glance." or "Backgrounding the (name of the story)."

9. Write a book review for a student publication about the newly released editions of *World Almanac,* or revised editions of *A Dictionary of American Slang,* or the new *Farmer's Almanac,* or the new edition of *Webster's International Dictionary.* You will have to "stylize" your review somehow to make it interesting.

10. For a local congressman or one of your state senators, trace his activities in Congress for recent months by researching him in *The Congressional Record.* Prepare an oral presentation,

not necessarily a written report. Or write an editorial endorsing him, praising him, or criticizing him on the basis of information you find.

11. Visit, as a staff or group, city hall or the courts or county seat offices to meet all the governmental officials, and particularly to inquire about their public records and access to them.

12. Trace any public figure (as a cabinet member or head of a huge corporation) through *Current Biography,* specialized biographical collections, such as *Who's Who,* to see what kind of impression you get of him through precise, fact-centered information. Or: What do the library reference sources say, in total, about your school?

13. From *Famous First Facts,* or a dictionary of dates and history, select an historic event of 50, 100, or 200 years ago. Then use the complete facilities of the reference library to write a feature story about it. Try to use the dramatic narrative as your style and structure if you can. Or for a season, or holiday, or special day, write a short feature about what has been said about it, using *Familiar Quotations* and other such collections for your material.

14. For every depth story, according to time availability, search the library for initial materials. Without fail, before giving your depth story to the editor, examine it for *primary* documentation you may have overlooked, or for details that need to be double-checked for accuracy.

FIVE DEPTH STORY IDEAS

You must be sure to explore RECREATION and LEISURE and ENTERTAINMENT when deciding upon depth ideas.

1. What will be the outlets for leisure time for the present student generation in its adult future, 20 years from now?

2. Have competitive team and group sports (football) become of secondary importance to students who seem to prefer private or small-group recreation (skiing)?

3. Is there a relationship between student enthusiasm for stopping environmental pollution and the increasing numbers who have taken to hiking, camping, canoeing during vacations?

4. What should be the fundamental purposes of physical education: fitness? development of recreational skills? exercise during the school day? preparing interscholastic athletes?

5. How does the *sedentary* nature of school equate with the naturally *active* student? Has television really produced in this student generation a group vastly different in habit and thought?

What Does It Mean? How Is It Done?

In December, 1965, the official monthly magazine for the Gannett Newspapers devoted an 18-page section to Reporting in Depth. In the introduction to the section, Editor Joseph N. Freudenberger commented: "Reporting in depth is being talked about increasingly. Editors and publishers like to boast about it. Reporters beg for time to do it. Journalism professors often recommend it. . . . But what is it?" In succeeding pages, editors and reporters from the Gannett Newspapers, mostly in New York State, provided their personal definitions, as well as advice and experience. Here, in a condensed text about depth reporting, are some of these comments.

"Now I know that a formal legislative meeting is frequently more imagined than real. They take the final, formal vote there and that's all. Much tinsel covers the chocolate. Proper coverage demands in-depth reporting. . . . Read all the legislation in advance and understand it. . . . Discuss the fare with leaders of both parties. . . . Watch out for caucuses. . . . Don't omit or gloss over what you don't understand. . . . In-depth reporting is an overworked phrase defining what we should all do regularly, but sometimes can't because of haste, space, ignorance or carelessness."

—Laurence J. Paul.

"What newspaper stories lack all too often nowadays is the accumulation of meaningful detail focused into a meaningful whole."

—Edward M. Kent.

"Reporting in depth is not identical to reporting at length. Some of the best depth pieces I have read have been relatively short. Yet, they tell the story; tell it well and interestingly. . . . Minutiae and trivia are not synonymous with depth. . . . If I were to reduce depth to one word, I think it would be insight."

—Alden Bracewell.

"The most important quality for the reporter, however, is detachment. When the research has been done and it is time to write, he must be able to stand back and stare at all this data, all this conflict, all this nonsense and decide what is the real goods and what is pap. Above all, he must have the objectivity to decide that a great deal of his material should be thrown away rather than imposed on the reader. If he has done a good job, there will be more discarded than used."

—Jack W. Germond.

". . . our belief that the coverage of board of education meetings does not stop with adjournment. It starts there. The reporter who wants to do in-depth reporting on boards of education often will find the best way is to go into the classroom. Look for himself. Listen and learn. Curiosity and sensitivity are good equipment to take with him. So is determination to push through educational jargon and routine resolutions to the people beyond."

—Kathleen A. Rowley.

"It's hard to get time to sit and really analyze issues. And this is most important to depth reporting—to sit, to think, to analyze. Another obstacle, present in any type of reporting, is a natural tendency for news sources to present only that news which puts them in a favorable light. But there's always someone—sooner or later—quite willing to talk."

—Bob Kostoff.

Chapter V

THE REPORTING

Student reporter Toni Karagosian was particularly interested in the new health fad of jogging. Everywhere, it seemed to her, somewhat corpulent men and women were sprouting in gray cotton warmup suits, plodding at half pace up streets, down alleys, across the park grounds. They could be heard coming, in a slap-slap of gym shoes on the asphalt, the sound of heavy breaths growing until they bobbed past in a swirl of warm air. Then at the same methodical pace—slap-slap—they dropped away into the distance, until specks on the horizon, the sound of shoes growing softer. Mostly, they were remarkable for the determined expressions and the persistent strides. Some could be heard on warm nights, through the open windows. Some more exhilarated in spirit could be known to awaken you in the morning. Six A.M. Slap-slap-slap. They brushed around you on sidewalks, and made those drivers not sure where their front fenders are swerve widely to miss them jogging along the gutter, slap-slap.

So Toni Karagosian began to think in terms of topic-lines:

Does jogging really do any good for those who want to lose weight?

Who (or what) is the person who gets involved in such a strenuous program?

Are there possibly as many negative health factors to jogging as there are positive?

When a reporter such as Toni begins to suffer the insistent mental

72

tugs of such questions, for her a story in depth cannot be far away.

The story begins most naturally at the local YMCA. There she finds her first heat of joggers. She finds a planned program already under way, complete with director and consultants and mimeographed brochures complete with success stories—and failures, too. Who are greater experts than the joggers themselves? That leads to a series of interviews about "why jogging?" About "how I got into jogging." About anecdotes and incidents that have made the lives of joggers perilous or humorous. She gets the theory of jogging from the director, and he promises to get statistics about YMCA joggers, locally and nationally.

One reporting session leads to another one. YMCA joggers give her names of do-it-myself, unorganized joggers. She checks the YWCA for the feminine viewpoint. She talks to a physical therapist of local reputation, to trainers for athletic teams. She talks to doctors. She talks to a wife who has a healthier, trimmer husband in the household. In other words, as a reporter she talks to everyone having any conceivable link with jogging. She even thinks to check with traffic police about accidents to, and safety hazards caused by, joggers.

But she is not satisfied. She has a notebook full of quotes, direct and indirect. That does not promise an effective story—this long listing of quotes that destroys so many depth stories. Worst of all stories is a stew of quotes; the columns of "he said's"; the collections of who said what, which perhaps could have been better presented as a tabulated list. She decides she still knows nothing about jogging. She cannot sense it, feel it, hate it. She must take up jogging herself. Through participation in the story, she begins to know jogging for the first time. She now has more than quotes to use. She has personal experience, descriptions, a sure sense of moods and pleasures. She jogs and interviews others at the same time, and this technique gives her description and dramatic narrative to weave into the long story. She begins to sound out others for slap-by-slap descriptions of their adventures as joggers. Her notebook swells. She begins to sense her subject. She has more material to write from. She even loses a couple of pounds.

Quotes; ideas; opinions.
Anecdotes and incidents and adventures.
Her own personal experiences.
Facts, statistics.

The reporter needs to complete one more area of reporting. Toni would like to know the origins and the history of jogging. She would like to know numbers of joggers in other areas, compared to her own. She would like to know of any disasters as well as overwhelming success stories. She would like to know of any systematic research by reputable sources into the results of jogging. That takes her to the libraries. She also makes a hopeful check of such agencies as the Department of Health, Education, and Welfare. She seeks other articles listed in the *Reader's Guide to Periodical Literature, The New York Times Index.* In those sources, she is careful NOT to steal information, style of writing, structures of stories, and anecdotes. She wants a surer grasp of her subject, not someone to write the story for her. Eventually, her notebook overflows; she cannot think of another resource for information; it is time to write the story before jogging is replaced by something else, maybe non-eating.

To report in depth, Toni did nothing unusual. She interviewed. She experienced and observed firsthand. She did whatever research and documentation possible. She leaned on experts to help her out. She became a somewhat-expert herself. (In her next depth story, she might become a semi-expert about environmental pollution.)

Depth reporting—like all reporting—is thorough, meticulous, exacting and time-involving. Just a great deal more of it than goes into the routine daily story.

Like all reporters, Toni has trouble getting enough precise facts—not just "several persons jog locally" but hard facts, such as "jogging groups in town report 320 joggers in their ranks, and that does not include unknown numbers of solitary, unorganized joggers." She wants to be sure to report all opinions about jogging, and she realizes there are *always more than two sides to report*. She is confounded by disagreement over basic ideas about jogging. When she cannot report agreement, she must report to the reader the disparity. She is reporting a story, not writing an editorial, so she tries to keep out of her story any slanted opinions of her own, or to launch an obvious crusade to sell the reader on jogging.

Because she has a long story to write, she tries especially hard to get anecdotes and incidents from her sources of information. "Well, will you try to recall for me, step by step, the confrontation you had with the angry old lady on Front Street?" She must be attentive, too, to descriptions. And she must try to interview people in their natural environment of jogging or getting ready to jog or recuperating on a green park bench afterward—all this to give a third dimension to her use of interviews. Not just WHAT was said, but HOW and WHEN and WHERE. She needs "environment" and dramatic sequences to brighten her story.

When Toni has exhausted her time allotment for the story, her sources of information, or herself, she turns to the writing—a difficult challenge to make thousands of words interesting without letup to thousands of readers. Her goal is to tell the readers everything interesting and important and very human about jogging so that when they put down their papers they feel a sense of completeness. Some may even take up jogging. Or steer clear of it—"Some nuts, these people!"

The jogging story with accompanying critique will be found at the end of this chapter.

The commercial reporters have turned in recent years more

and more to depth reporting, paying less and less attention to routine news such as bulletin-board announcements, fender-benders, and routine personal items.

Editors of the Associated Press, the largest news-gathering organization in the world, in 1967 announced their belief in the depth report—what they called "the submerged dimension" in the news. Teams of reporters (more than one person can be assigned to a depth story) produced 268 such stories in one year. *Life* magazine long has led in depth reporting. In October, 1969, to do a depth report about M-Day (Moratorium Day, to protest the war in Vietnam), *Newsweek* magazine got a total of 200,000 words from all its bureaus and correspondents and stringers in the United States, plus 30 special campus correspondents. All this was condensed into one "cover story" in depth.

For the now-defunct *Saturday Evening Post,* depth reporting was called "enterprise reporting." One managing editor referred to it as "the genius of all good journalism." The stories were called "Acts." He continued in his comments:

"I have never been overly impressed with another magazine's boast that it can come out with a major article with pictures in color in three days. Some of our major articles require months of preparation. I believe absolutely that enterprise reporting is the genius of successful journalism. By the phrase, I mean the kind of investigative reporting that requires the reporter to do whatever, to go wherever is necessary—by bathysphere or sailplane—to get the facts. Truth must be his central idea. If he stirs controversy in the process, it must be with responsibility and without bias. Of course, every honest reporter works this way, whether he is uncovering corruption in his local city hall, telling the story of Mississippi blacks, or writing on poverty in Harlem. All we ask of our writers is to tell us what the facts are."

It was the great editor of *The Wall Street Journal,* Bernard Kilgore, who most persistently urged reporting in depth and who most perceptively declared, on several occasions, its significance to journalism: "The newspaper of the future must become an instrument of intellectual leadership, an institution of intellectual development—a center of learning."

To Do, to Read, to Think About

1. For depth stories that start on page 1 of *The Wall Street Journal,* study carefully these points:

- The ways the reporter operated.
- The kinds of detail he accumulated.
- The degree of his personal involvement.

Make note of anything detrimental, such as editorial bias, or too-generalized facts, or unsupported conclusions and opinions. How has the reporter avoided a story that is mostly a listing of quoted information?

2. For additional guidance to techniques of reporting, refer to *The Student Journalist and Common Story Assignments* and *The Student Journalist and Creative Writing* (Richards Rosen Press).

3. For a depth story topic-line (see Chapter III), outline as fully as you can all the reporting resources you can use, whether documents or persons or events. Then once the reporting gets under way, be especially alert to asking your sources for suggestions of additional places and persons to check. Plan for (1) Research, (2) Interviewing, (3) Observation by yourself, and (4) perhaps Personal Involvement. Be certain to list "external" sources—such as wives of joggers who may be better sources for information than the joggers themselves; or those who quit jogging and are more quotable than those who stick to it, or sporting goods dealers who may have an interesting report about sudden, increased sales in fluorescent sweatsuits.

4. During an interview, how can you tell if the person is giv-

ing you false or misleading information—or covering up details? How can you verify and validate such doubtful information?

5. "Jogging" would be a story taken from popular culture; what other depth stories are brought to mind? Too many depth stories are devoted to politics; not enough explore the public fascination with popular culture.

FIVE DEPTH STORY IDEAS

You must be sure you explore the CULTURAL aspects of student life.

1. The Vice-President of the United States claimed rock lyrics advertised the drug culture—what is the truth about philosophy, psychology, and life-style advanced by popular lyrics (The Beatles, others)?

2. How serious are the collisions of youth culture with school standards—mod clothes vs. dress codes, rock music vs. music taught in classes, levels of taste vs. student publications, Salinger (the novelist, J. D.) vs. literature courses?

3. What all is there to report about _____, the newest of fads and fashions in the student generation?

4. What were the identifiable, new, distinct life-styles of the present middle generation, which so often stands against the life-style of students—and what from that time to this has become a more permanent part of American life-style? The crewcut? Big band music? Zoot suit? Or what have students today discarded that was unique to the present middle generation of Americans?

5. How much is the student generation the victim of commercialization of fads and fashions (such as maxiskirts of 1970)? How much profit is there to selling changing cultures and life-styles?

Also: examine carefully all the shibboleths about the present student generation: don't read . . . more violent . . . against the work ethic . . . lower standards of taste, etc.

A Critique of a Story to Study: Jogging

Toni Karagosian falls into a too-common trap, after all, for the depth reporter. She is overwhelmed by her book of quotes. She has talked to so many people and they have said so many things of interest, she has been unable to whittle away most of them. She tries to jam too many of them into her story so it sounds like a panel discussion. She needs to better summarize quoted matter.

She must make something more of her quotes than a listing. She might select one typical person as the "central subject" of the story—called the **CASE-STUDY** method of telling a story. In telling all about him and letting him be quoted fully, she may be able to ignore most of the others interviewed. One person typical of the many. Then she could have referred to other persons only when they disagree or have other, varying experiences to report.

Too, she could have **categorized** all her quotes and information. Those seeking to lose poundage in one category. Those who want to enliven their vital processes with exercise in another. The failures in one section of the story; the successes in another. Those health faddists seeking a new fad. Those for jogging; those against. The problems of jogging. The pleasant experiences. The whimsical experiences. Thus, if she had to use many persons in her story, at least the subject matter would fall into easily tracked categories. Her story would then have been "blocked."

She could have eliminated a great many direct quotes by **synthesizing** them. Rather than use 30 words reporting, in direct quote, this:

"I prefer running in the country, up and down hills, where scenery is not so monotonous. I like to see the cows, and hear the birds chirping," said Young.

She could have synthesized all that and other similar comments into this statement, an indirect quote:

> Joggers in Reno have preferences. One likes to run in the country to see the cows. Another likes . . . (and so on).

By cutting down on the amount of space given to rather repetitious quotes and comments from 13 joggers (it gets to be a parade whizzing before the reader's eyes), she could have brought in more factual information, more description of joggers and jogging, more anecdotes and incidents, and perhaps some of her own sensory perceptions of jogging. She as a reporter had plenty of such material to use.

Her lead section is a little long. She could have cut it one third at least before she got to her first definite human interest point—about the four research chemists.

She could have done more with the outside contacts with joggers—the sporting goods dealer with his fluorescent sweatsuits designed for traffic safety. That point has great possibilities, leading right to the door, too, of the traffic bureau.

Most of all, her reporting was excellent. But in transferring her notes to a written story—like most starting reporters—she did not see clearly enough from the outset a pattern by which the story could be told.

. . . With unending fascination for the reader, who probably had not jogged at all.

The Story

From *The Sagebrush,* University of Nevada, Reno.

Fat and thin, young and old, with sweating foreheads, burning throats and heaving chests, you see them huffing, puffing and bouncing up and down hills through the parks, the desert and the city streets.

They are members of a new American breed, the Joggers, participating in one of their favorite forms of outdoor recreation, one of the most popular physical fitness programs today.

The joggers now are a part of the daily scene in such areas as Virginia Lake, Washoe County Golf Course, Wingfield and Idle-wild Parks, the University of Nevada Reno Campus and the hills in the country.

And this growing sport has proved so fruitful it is even a benefit for those part-time athletes who still prefer to walk than run—it is great for speeding up a round of golf: Golf-and-Jog is the name of the game dubbed in by one golfer.

Jogging is a simple type of exercise requiring no highly developed skills nor special equipment. Its great appeal is that it is so handy. Almost anyone can do it anywhere, and it's free. All that is needed are old clothes and comfortable shoes.

To the world's champion distance walker, jogging has a certain reverie about it. This enthusiast solves his problems, thinks about God and nature, and sings while he jogs.

The ranks of jogging enthusiasts include professors, students, professional men. They run early in the morning, late in the night, in the afternoon, either indoors or outdoors.

Four research chemists employed by the U.S. Bureau of Mines, located on the university campus, go jogging together every day. Oscar Winget, Dave MacDonald, Don Bauer, and Ken Broad-head began jogging on their lunch hour in September.

Winget, 37, said they start right from the side door of the Mines building. In good weather several of them also ride their bikes to work.

Broadhead, 39, said he had been thin all his life and when he started to gain weight he knew it was time to do something about it. He is a scoutmaster and said it looked bad when the boys would out-hike him.

When the four started jogging he said they got many strange looks, but now do not feel self-conscious at all. They follow a two-mile route which takes about 15 minutes.

Jogging has the advantage of two good exercises in one—run-

ning and walking. It is an easy, slow-paced run alternated with breath-catching periods of walking. For example, some beginners jog 55 yards and walk 55 yards. Then as they continue to run they increase the jogging and decrease the walking periods.

The choice of place and time for jogging is up to each individual. Most remain unorganized, preferring to run at their own speed, where and when they choose, and perhaps undetected. Like any other physical conditioning program, it must be continued for its greatest benefits.

Washoe District Court Judge Grant L. Bowen said he took up jogging because he was overweight and needed strenuous physical exercise. He has been jogging for three years, lost about 30 pounds and his normal pulse rate has dropped from 80 to between 40 and 45.

Judge Bowen feels he is in good physical shape now and also enjoys other physical activities such as golf, hunting, and skiing. He follows various routes ranging from three to nine and one-half miles, spending 40 to 50 minutes a day jogging.

When running he says he is detached from how far he has left to go, but instead his mind is at work solving problems and getting ready for the following day.

Cross-country walking champion Byron Young, Sparks, began jogging with the idea of influencing people to eat better, and now jogs 10 to 15 miles at a time just to keep in shape.

To illustrate the depth story about jogging, student photographer Mike Perry was sent out to record on film the same persons reporter Toni Kuragosian was recording in words. Mike jogged along, click matching step. He was particularly intent on showing the paradox between joggers-in-sweatsuits and ordinary, everyday scenes in the community. Thus, noon joggers coming out of the university building where they taught. Joggers striding down main street past the gas signs and over the hot asphalt. Jogger pacing through the neighborhood with his dog, slightly overweight, in sympathetic stride right behind him. Joggers alone would not have made suitable illustrations. Joggers against environment—another dimension completely.

To prove his point of what physical fitness will do for a person he set the record for walking cross-country last year. Young has been jogging for over two and one-half years and is now considering an attempt to break the nonstop run-walk (jogging) record of 121 miles.

"I prefer running in the country, up and down hills, where the scenery is not so monotonous. I like to see the cows and hear the birds chirping," says Young.

"While jogging my mind is clear and active solving my problems. Because my mind is uninterrupted I can memorize twice as fast as normally. I also think of God and nature while I jog," he says. Since he has good breath control, he practices singing while he jogs.

Young, who is also a professional bowler and tennis player, says jogging conditions a person to do all types of activities better. He feels it is the older person who needs jogging more, and yet the younger are most responsive to it. Perhaps they are less self-conscious.

He cautions people never to run right after eating since it increases the chance of having a heart attack, because nearly half of a person's blood is being used for digestion.

Young feels that every human being should exercise to some extent because physically fit citizens would make for a better and healthier nation.

Mrs. Tom Craven, athletic director at the Reno YWCA, says there are 14 women and several students who jog regularly for a physical fitness program which the Y offers three times a week. Any woman interested in jogging can still join the program.

Keith Jones, a floorman at a local casino, has been jogging regularly for two years because it keeps him in good shape. He runs two miles a day, six days a week. When he started out he said people thought he was crazy, but several of his neighbors did run with him, although most of them have since stopped jogging.

Dr. Allen J. Belkind, assistant professor of English, began

jogging when he saw so many people in his neighborhood of Idlewild Park doing it. He has been jogging now for about two years and runs one to one and one-half miles twice a week.

He thinks jogging is an enjoyable exercise, and it also cuts down the tensions of academic life. He doubts if jogging is too widespread through the faculty, but feels it would be a perfect exercise for the deadly, indoor aspects of academic life.

Dr. George A. Cann, Reno physician, believes jogging is an excellent physical exercise. He feels it is most important for a prospective jogger to have a physical check-up before he begins exercising.

If a person is in good condition, his age will make no difference. Dr. Cann will tell these people, who do not have heart trouble, to go ahead and jog, but to start gradually and build up to long distances.

"Jogging helps take off weight, is good exercise for the heart muscle, and helps the circulation," says Dr. Cann.

Although a jogger needs no special equipment, there are various items he might consider. Most popular with joggers are sweatshirts and sweatpants. Sauna suits, which are made of rubberized material, cause perspiration to increase and help those who are running to lose weight.

Dr. Art Broten, chairman of the university's department of health and physical education, agreed wholeheartedly with physician Cann.

"Jogging is an excellent form of exercise for the person who has no serious physiological disorders. But like any other form of exercise, it must be approached with common sense.

"The individual must use moderation to build up to long distances. There are no doubts that it is beneficial, and to most people it is fun. Just being outside is beneficial, and jogging instills pride in being able to build up to longer distances."

Broten explained that jogging is not a muscle-building exercise like weight lifting. "Weights build up power, while jogging enhances the circulatory system." He said there is a group of faculty members who have been meeting for about three years to work out.

"They jog, skip rope, use the weights and practice gymnastics, alternating so it doesn't get monotonous. It is more fun with a group, the social aspect and kidding are part of the fun."

One sporting goods store recently sold bright yellow and fluorescent sweatsuits so joggers can be seen by passing cars, since so many run early in the mornings or at dusk.

Several types of jogging shoes with various thicknesses of soles are sold for both indoor and outdoor use. A variety of weighted equipment is also made which the jogger can wear around his waist to help take off inches. It weighs from five to ten pounds.

A jogger can also put weighted inner soles in his shoes, or ankle weights over his shoes, to help build up leg muscles. Some wear sweat bands around the forehand.

A modest husband-and-wife running team, who did not wish to give their names but believe in speeding up a round of golf, jog regularly around Virginia Lake. He is 51 and has been jogging on and off for seven years. His wife, 47, is a beginner, and jogs 50 paces and walks 50 paces.

He uses bowling shoes, which he has found very suitable. Both run to keep in shape and feel it's given them endurance that may come in handy in any emergency. They have lost a few pounds each, but more important they are holdng their weight.

He said this winter has been bad for joggers around the lake because it was either too muddy or full of snow, and now there are deep ruts. He would like to see a jogging path made around Virginia Lake, which is one mile in circumference.

"When we go golfing now, we often take only a few clubs and jog to our golf balls each time. It is great for speeding up play. I wish more people would try it." (The story needs a stronger ending.)

Reliability of the News

The National Observer, a weekly national newspaper from Washington, D.C., has been deeply concerned about keeping faith with—and from—its readers. Sweeping changes to ensure reliability are not necessary, editors of *The National Observer* wrote in July, 1970. But in every story, reporters/writers are urged to pay attention to little improvements. The editors listed these points as good advice for establishing credibility in news reports:

1. Clearly label all opinion articles as such. Readers tend to confuse the opinions of columnists with reports of opinions carried in news accounts.

2. Let the reader know the writer's credentials. If a writer about Vietnam has been there many times, his reports could carry more weight with the reader than those commentators who have not.

3. Correct errors. Many persons contend that things they know are wrong in news stories never are set right.

4. Print all shades of opinion in letters to the editor.

5. Print a story at enough length to give the ins and outs of the controversy and to present all contrasting viewpoints.

6. View events and personalities—as a reporter/writer—with skepticism but never with venom.

7. Clearly identify the sources of information in an article by specific names rather than as "unidentified."

Chapter VI

THE WRITING

A story in depth usually is too long to be carried by the straight news form—unless you have a preponderance of impressive facts, like a machine gun burst of bullets to keep the reader awake and alert. For the depth story, you must turn in part to the techniques of the essayist and the short-story writer. Episodes. Dramatic narrative. Dialogue. Bright style. Built-in suspense. You must work with blocks of material, not just with sentences of factual information strung together. You must work with incidents and anecdotes, with action interviews involving dialogue and description. You must work with examples and illustrations, and with narrated sequences of action.

As well as with facts.

For instance, you might not begin a depth story with a fact lead adhering to the golden principles of the 5 W's-and-H like this:

> The survival of several nearly extinct species of animals depends upon their successfully breeding in captivity in zoos, such as the Bronx Zoo where staff member Donald Bruning has been repeatedly disappointed by failure.

Nothing wrong with that kind of straightforward, one-sentence, fact-centered, mood-divorced lead. The question is: Will it support a long story? The quick fact-lead quickly dissipates its power —like the 100-yard dash runner. It doesn't develop enough suspense or promise of reward to send a reader, relaxed and ready to read, into the long article.

Here is another kind of lead more effective for the needs of depth stories: the narrative lead as used by Neal Ulman of *The Wall Street Journal*. It extends several paragraphs before it comes to a logical conclusion—or is it fulfillment?—like the introduction to an essay or short story.

NEW YORK—When Donald Bruning arrived at his Bronx Zoo office one morning last month, he found that a keeper had placed on his desk a small blue egg. Mr. Bruning's heart sank.

Twenty days earlier, when the egg was laid, Mr. Bruning had taken it from the nest and put it in one of the bird department's mechanical incubators. The machine periodically rotated the egg to prevent a dangerous adhesion of the embryo to its shell, but Mr. Bruning, a curatorial trainee, turned it daily himself, just to make sure. Each time, he sprayed it with a humidifier. And recently he had taken to holding the shell to his ear, to catch the first sounds of hatching.

All for naught. An incomplete perforation around the top of the shell—the usual exit point for the emerging creature—signaled another failure in the zoo's six-year effort to raise a White-faced Glossy Ibis in captivity. The embryo had twisted its neck while pecking open the shell during the night, and it had died before it could hatch.

A few years ago such an untimely demise might have been taken in stride. But the Bronx Zoo, and other such installations around the nation, now regard their breeding programs with urgent concern. Zoos, once looked on as diverting collections of strange creatures, are fast becoming the last refuge for a lengthening list of wild creatures. Some kinds of bison, deer and wild horses exist only in captivity today, and many other creatures are becoming almost as rare. As the depredations of man continue to crowd out the animals, zoos are taking on a new significance for the preservation of wilderness creatures.

Once his introduction is set down, as you can see, the writer moves on to explore his topic-line fully. Here is the literature to journalism, coupling the talent of reporting with the genius of writing.

Extended leads. An episode narrated in its sequence of action. Dialogue. A descriptive passage heavy with mood.

A short lead is possible if it has enough crash and impact to it to jolt the reader into wide-eyed attention. Such as this one that shakes up the smoker:

> For R. J. Reynolds Tobacco Company, the "wages of sin" are about $1.5 million.

Thus, in writing the depth story, the initial problem is visualizing an introduction that explains the topic-line; sets the proper mood; gets across the who, what, when, where, why, how; and yet interests the reader profoundly. Without arousing that interest—well, you might as well give the rest of your allotted room on the page to white space.

The next problem of writing the depth story is keeping the reader moving ahead. Long and needless paragraphs of description can turn him away, just as assuredly as they do in *Vanity Fair,* a prime example of long-winded Victorian style and structure. Tangled sentences slow him down. Dull statistics and unimportant facts bore him. Technical information not made clear confounds him. Long black blocks of unbroken type unsettle him —a formidable challenge to overcome rather than a pleasant reading experience to savor. All that will discourage the reader.

So: A depth story requires the time to write and to rewrite and to edit. It must be meticulously written for clear, concise prose. It must be edited to strike out all unnecessary, repetitive, or irrelevant information. It must be sounded for boring spots or slowdown points, to be taken out or rewritten. It must be groomed, crafted, curried, hand-fashioned, shined, and rubbed, until the story is near-perfect in readability.

Once the lead (or introduction) is set down, you the writer can consciously use other time-tested techniques to hold reader interest. Here are five possibilities:

1. Using examples and illustrations

Don't tell the reader that Needles, California, is one of the hottest communities in the United States. Give him the startling statistics to make him feel the heat. Better, compare the facts to those of your own (and the reader's) locality. And "show him" how hot it is by illustration, as did Bill Sluis for *The Wall Street Journal.*

So the roads outside of town are dotted with overheated cars. Tourists burn their fingers on searing radiator caps. Their barefoot children step out on the highway and suffer blisters. Pets pass out, a veterinarian explained, because the temperature inside a parked car can reach almost 200 degrees in 15 minutes—even with one window open.

Needles residents know how to take care of their pets, however. [*Now the illustrations.*] One man air-conditioned his garage for the sole benefit of his dog. A local rodeo cowboy has discovered a cheaper solution. He dresses his black hound in a dirty, sagging T-shirt; then he hoses down the dog, and the shirt keeps the moisture from evaporating rapidly. If the cowboy isn't around, Old T shirt (the dog's name) hurls himself into a handy irrigation ditch.

A reporter must train himself to think from the *general* to the *specific*. Then he can direct the reader accordingly. If the person interviewed says generally:

"Plenty hot in the summer around here."

The reporter wants something more specific:

"How hot?"

"Oh, over hundred degrees most days."

Still not specific enough for the reporter who wants to move from the general to the specific:

"Well, exactly how hot is over a hundred degrees?"

"Average midday temperature around here in the summer months is 125 degrees. Hottest we ever had was 137."

"What happens? Can you think of some good examples of what happens when it gets to be 125?"

Then come the illustrations and examples.

The reverse, of course, is going from the specific to the general. From the specific facts or specific examples to their generalized, overall meaning and interpretation.

2. Inserting anecdotes

When you are deep in the story and you want to bring in a new point you can start with—an anecdote. Instead of starting a new section about wiretapping this way:

Wiretapping is so easily done that even those officials who wiretap for evidence get uneasy.

You could start, for reviving interest, with a good story, like this:

A reporter called up a Department of Justice official in Washington to get details about wiretapping and asked:

"What's your opinion about all this wiretapping?"

The official answered. "Well, I can't tell you that over this phone!"

As spurious as that anecdote sounds, now making the rounds in Washington, D.C., it does come near to the truth about the ease, frequency, and "cross-indexing" of wiretapping today.

(Then can follow facts and opinions about wiretapping.)

Anecdotes are more artificial than examples and illustrations, but they serve important functions as revivalists.

3. Enlivening quotes

It is one thing to report in straightforward style what a person says, like this:

The King, head of the Black Disciples, said, "You live the

old-style life—the way the older folks live—and you wind up looking like you're 50 when you're 30."

But if you pay careful attention to *how* it was said to you, *where* it was said, *in what environment,* and as part of a sequence of actions and *dialogue,* you can report the quote in a much more interesting and meaningful manner, like this:

The King, a muscular 22-year-old grade school dropout with a lengthy police record, sprawls across a chair in the shabby storefront headquarters of the Black Disciples, a street gang he leads—and the source of his royal title. "Getting together is the thing, you know," he muses. "That's what's going to get us away from lousy jobs and apartments that aren't fit to live in. You live the old-style life—the way the older folks do —and you wind up looking like you're 50 when you're 30."

More information is included; the reader learns more.
As well as becoming more interested.
To get this kind of information, you must interview a person in *his* natural environment, and you must do more than take notes on answers. You must observe how he says it, as well as study consciously the environment.

4. Giving meaning to facts

Some facts are better presented in charts and graphs and listings. Such as this start of a listing about World's Fairs:

City	Date	Acreage	No. of exhibits	Attendance
London	1851	26	13,939	6,039,195
Paris	1900	336	80,000	39,000,000
London	1951	—	—	18,000,000
New York	1964–5	646	—	—

Try to explain that in prose style.

Wants Lottery System

Nixon Proceeds To Revise Draft

PROBLEMS! PROBLEMS!—Every young male who reaches eighteen is faced with the problem of military service. Should he wait until he is drafted and serve two years in the Army? Or, should he volunteer and serve either three or four years in the branch of his choice. Senior John Scott hears an explanation of the benefits of the Air Force from Little Rock recruiter, Sgt. Bill Thorne.

Sweeping revisions in the U.S. Selective Service System are in the process of being made by President Richard Nixon.

Revisions that he has undertaken during the past two months have included:

● Partial suspension of the draft for October and complete suspension for November and December.

● Requesting that Congress abolish the present Selective Service System and establish a national lottery system.

● Firing Gen. Lewis B. Hershey as head of the Selective Service System. Gen. Hershey had been head of the System since it was established in 1941.

Shows 'Faith'

President Nixon ordered the three-month suspension of the draft on September 19. He indicated at the time that the suspension was being ordered "to show the need for revisions in the Selective Service System."

Under his partial suspension order for October, 29,000 men were ordered for induction during the month. However, only 10,000 were actually inducted. 10,000 were given a one-month delay, and 9,000 were given a two-month delay.

No men will be called for induction in November and December except those who were granted extension as part of the 29,000 called in October.

Wants Lottery

President Nixon wants Congress to establish a national lottery system for the draft.

Under his proposed system, which is currently being debated in Congress and which is expected to pass, only 19 year old men would be inducted.

Names of all 19 year olds in the nation would be placed in a container, located in Washington, and names would be drawn monthly to fill draft calls.

Boards Function For Registration

Males must register for the draft within five days after reaching eighteen.

Registering places in Little Rock are Local Boards 60 and 61, located in the Federal Office Building at 700 West Capitol.

Federal laws provide severe penalties to males who fail to register within five days of reaching eighteen.

If a young man's name had not been drawn by the time of his 20th birthday, his name would be removed from the lottery and he would no longer be eligible for the draft, except in cases of "extreme national emergency."

Gen. Lewis B. Hershey, head of the Selective System until dismissal this month, had repeatedly indicated his disapproval of a national lottery system.

Regardless of whether President Nixon's proposed legisla-tion for a national lottery is passed by Congress, the President has announced that he will use his executive powers to order Selective Service System to draft only men who are 19 years old.

However, a 19 year old who seeks deferment to attend college would receive one and would report to service after graduation from college or upon his withdrawal from college.

Secretary of Defense Melvin Laird is supporting Nixon's draft plan.

History Reveals Problems With Methods of Selection For United States Military

By LARRY REEVES

Throughout history the U. S. has had difficulty in drafting men to meet its military needs.

During the American Revolution, the War of 1812, the U. S.-Mexican War of 1847, and the Indian uprisings in the West, there was no form of compulsory military service and the Army had to depend entirely on volunteers.

Conscription Appears

The first form of a compulsory draft—then called conscription—appeared during the Civil War. Both the Federal Government and the Confederacy adopted it.

But, laws provided substitutions for service, bounties, and large scale exemptions that caused the conscription system to be a failure.

In 1927—one year after U.S. entry into World War 1—Congress passed a Selective Service Act that authorized "a selective draft" for all citizens between 21 and 31 years of age for service during the duration of the national emergency.

Sets Limitations

The Act prohibited bounties, substitutions, or exemptions except for ministers, divinity students, elected state and national officials, and men engaged in essential occupations. The Act expired at the end of World War 1.

In 1940—the date of U.S. entry in World War II—Congress passed another Selective Service System Act, which also provided for a draft during peacetime.

The 1940 Act, with minor revisions, governs today's Selective Service System.

Gen. Lewis B. Hershey was appointed by President Franklin D. Roosevelt to establish and supervise the Selective Service System. He served as head until he was fired this month by President Nixon.

The methods used to draft men in the U.S. have received criticism each time they were employed, especially during the Korean Conflict of the 1950's and the Viet Nam Conflict of the 60's.

'Nixon Suspension Will Affect Quota,' Major Ray Says

By CHERIE JOHNSON

"President Nixon's suspension of the draft will greatly affect Arkansas," Major Middleton P. Ray, chief of the manpower division of the Arkansas Selective Service System, said.

Major Ray said that Arkansas' quota of the 29,000 to be inducted nationally in October is 137.

Some Extended

He indicated that only 68 would actually report in October and that, in accordance with Nixon's order to grant an extension to part of the inductees, 69 would report in November.

"As of yet, no draft call has been issued for December," he said.

Major Ray said that he expected revisions will be made in the Selective Service System in December. "Probably, they will be major revisions," he said.

Sees Reduction

As President Nixon continues to withdraw troops, there will be sharp reductions in the number of men called to duty, according to Major Ray.

He said that Arkansas has had no difficulty in meeting its draft quotas during the past years.

"It is always necessary to call nearly as twice as many men to take physical and mental examinators than are inducted," he said, explaining that "quite a few" flunk either the physical or mental test, or both.

Major Ray said that there had been "very few" cases of men refusing to be inducted.

"As a whole, our operations have been smooth," he said.

Issue of the Issue

Draft System: New Revisions

Criticisms of Selective Service Relate Closely to Asian Conflict

Closely associated with criticisms of the draft system is criticisms of the Viet Nam Conflict.

"You can't separate one from the other," Sen. Eugene McCarthy of Minnesota contends.

Expresses Belief

Sen. McCarthy believes that if America were not involved in Viet Nam, "it would "greatly reduce" the number of young men needed for the Armed Forces and thus would reduce criticisms of the draft whether it employed its present methods of calling men or a national lottery as proposed by President Nixon.

Sen. McCarthy was one of slightly more than one million Americans who displayed their opposition to American involvement in Viet Nam on October 15, designated as "Moratorium Day."

Though the one million who demonstrated October 15 represented less than one-half of the U.S. population, it did display that America has a great deal of dissent in regard to Viet Nam.

Nixon Unmoved

However, President Nixon indicated that he would not be swayed by the Moratorium and that he would not change his policies in regard to Viet Nam.

"I will not be the first U.S. President to lose a war," Nixon asserted.

And, for creating public support for Nixon's Viet Nam policies, the Moratorium did just that.

Prior to the Moratorium, only 37 per cent of the American people, according to Gallup Poll, supported Nixon's policies on Viet Nam. A week after the Moratorium, 61 per cent of the American people indicated approval of Nixon's policies.

Is It Temporary?

Yet, many veteran politicians believe that American support of Nixon's policies are only temporary, and unless he continues to withdraw troops and shows that he is leading the nation to a peaceful settlement, the support will be withdrawn.

The number of well-known American men and women who oppose the Viet Nam Conflict and want American withdrawal is growing. These people include Sen. J. W. Fulbright, Sen. Martin Luther King, Sen. Kennedy, Helen Hayes, Paul Newman, Mayor John Lindsey, and Ralph Abernathy.

And, most of those who oppose the Viet Nam Conflict are the sharpest critics of the Selective Service System.

Pupils Oppose Draft's System But Support Handling of War

Students at Central are overwhelmingly opposed to the present methods used in drafting men, but they give support for America's involvement in Viet Nam.

Of 200 students interviewed at random, 80 per cent (160) indicated they felt present Selective Service System laws should be changed. Eighteen per cent (36) said they should not be changed and two per cent (4) had no opinion.

Support Involvement

In regard to Viet Nam, 64 per cent (or 128 students) said they supported American involvement in Viet Nam.

Thirty-six per cent opposed involvement in Viet Nam. None of the 200 polled gave a "no opinion" answer, a rarity in Tiger polls.

Further questioning on the draft showed that only 55 students out of the 200 thought the U.S. should abolish its draft system and operate its Armed Forces on a volunteer basis.

Individual students comments on both the draft and Viet Nam indicated sharp differences of opinions.

Student body president John Peace, who supports Nixon's policies on Viet Nam, believes that there should be a draft system where the bulk of men would be volunteers.

Ronald Sterling believes a revised system of the draft is needed and that "it is taking too long" to bring about "needed revisions."

Girl Wants Withdrawal

"The draft should be abolished and the U.S. should withdraw immediately from Viet Nam," Debbie Olson said.

However, Cindy Mackin believes that the U.S. should not leave Viet Nam until "we can leave honorably and insure peace for the people of Viet Nam."

Cindy, along with Frances Caldwell, support President Nixon's proposal for a national draft lottery.

November 14, 1969   LITTLE ROCK CENTRAL HIGH TIGER   Page 7

Issue of the Issue

Merits of Mayor's Council

City Forms Mayor's Council To Learn Problems of Youth

By CHERIE JOHNSON

NAMED FOR HIM—Little Rock Mayor Mann Boyd was one of the chief instigators and is an active supporter of the Mayor's Youth Council, a group of teenagers who are attempting to bridge the gap between city government and the city's youth. The Council has fulfilled several projects and is now attempting to gain a large, citywide youth recreation center.

An Editorial

Council Can Assist Youths If It Seeks Practical Goal

Chairman for Mayor's Council Says City Needs Youth Facility Which Has Supervised Events

By MICHAEL BABB

RICK CAMPBELL
Council Chairman

Two Get Offices On Youth Council

Only 24 in 100 Give Support

Pupils Show Little Interest in Council's Work

NONSCHOOL NEWS? Just about everything touches the student. The school is part of the community. Education is not remote from the experiences of the world. All those points shape the news policies of the staff of the Little Rock Central High Tiger. *For every issue, one in-depth page is planned and reported. Here, in late 1969 on the eve of switching to a draft lottery, a full page is devoted to stories, surveys, and interviews about The Draft. A background piece about the President's plans, a history of the draft system, an interview with a selective service official, a random survey among students, a résumé of criticisms of the draft system —all of these stories are* **packaged** *into one page, one topic explored in depth. All of this information could have been worked into one long story, but it would have been difficult to write, to read, to display. Thus—packaging as a better technique. Above: a community story.*

A news photograph many times doesn't need words . . . as in this case, timers and runner pictured at 1/500 of a second at the finish line. Depth photographers, as well as reporters/writers, must be used to cover news in

Facts can also be made more meaningful to readers by fitting them into a familiar frame of reference. Why write this:

By the end of 1969 Americans killed in battle in Vietnam numbered 36,866; those wounded 119,376.

When you can make meaningful, more impactful comparisons such as these:

By the end of 1969, Americans killed in battle in Vietnam numbered 36,866—the equivalent of every person in such cities as Port Huron, Michigan, Newport, Rhode Island, or Waukesha, Wisconsin. The number wounded were 119,376— the population of Topeka, Kansas.

Another point about facts—cover ground as fast as possible. You do not need to attribute all facts as long as you know they are accurate.

5. *Using the narrative*

Facts listed without variation get dull, unless the facts consistently are startling. Direct quotes from interviews listed without interruption or variation get dull, like an uninspired monologue. Therefore, to present such information in a brighter style of writing, you can turn to the dramatic narrative, which includes facts, quotes, description, chronological order, and action —all objective material—in a pattern interesting to the reader.

For instance, the following short narrative. Notice its distinguishing characteristics as numbered in boldface in the story itself:

1. *The lead,* or introduction, to the story must try to catch the reader's interest. Here by CONTRAST—greatest hoax now in unpretentious hole. It is a "statement" lead.

2. *The narrative* contains description, factual information, direct quotes, sequence of action . . . told exactly as it was said and as it was seen.

3. Now, a switch to purely *factual information*—here, historical information about the hoax. The narrative is dropped for a few paragraphs, a kind of flashback.

4. A *transition* brings the reader back to the narrative: "So the question of a visitor" (really the reporter). . . . Transitions must be included to direct the reader clearly from one part of the narrative story to another.

5. A concluding anecdote to bring the narrative to a close on a strong impression . . . *an ending* to be remembered, not quickly forgotten. An anecdote serves this purpose admirably.

Here is the full story:

Cooperstown, New York

(1) The latest home for the most sensational hoax of the 19th century—the Cardiff Giant—is an unpretentious hole in the ground here, scarcely 100 miles from where it was unearthed in 1869 at Cardiff, N.Y.

A tanned, leathery employee of the Farmer's Museum at Cooperstown last week narrated the recant history of the Giant as he chipped away dirt from its gypsum carcass. "Oh, a few people still come in here just to see the Cardiff Giant," he said. "And, you know, quite a lot I talk to very old ladies who still swear by it."

(2) With a spade he sliced away winter's decay from the feet of the statue. They were twisted to the side, putting the Giant into a slightly embryonic position. "When the Giant first came here . . . let me see, I can't quite remember when, guess it was in '47 . . . people packed in to see him. They threw money—dimes, quarters, nickels—into the pit, and we had no trouble getting boys to clean it out. Now, no one will do it."

He went on with the grooming and the story.

(3) Two men planned the hoax. They had the Giant—12 feet high—carved from gypsum imported from Iowa. The statue was seasoned with acid and buried on a farm 12 miles south of Syracuse, N.Y. A year later (1869) it was "accidentally" discovered and unearthed.

Speculation at the time was rife. It was a petrified man and proved that giants once walked the Earth, claimed Biblical experts. It was the mummy of a giant Indian prophet who had predicted the coming of the white man, said others. It was Lot's wife. It was a statue erected centuries before by Jesuit missionaries. The Giant, enormous in fame, was displayed throughout the East and the Midwest. Even P. T. Barnum got into the act. He ordered an exact duplicate made in plaster and displayed it at his museum in New York.

(4) So the question of a visitor to the Farmer's Museum was natural. "Which Cardiff Giant is this?" he asked, a little too sarcastically.

The employee put down his spade, stepped onto the Giant's thigh, and eyed the inquisitor. "Oh, you're one of those guys!" He laughed. "No, this is the genuine Cardiff Giant."

He toed the cracks where the Giant's legs had broken off at the knees. "Yes, sir, at the dedication here, just a mob of people. We couldn't possibly hold them back. They just had to see the famous Giant." He looked down at the sleeping stone man, half-buried in the dirt wash of spring thaws and rains. "I always tell the schoolchildren that here is the only thing in the whole museum that is a fake. It really should be in the Fenimore Museum across the road . . . folk art, you know. But it *was* found on a farm."

At Cooperstown, therefore, the Giant is a marvel to old-timers, an amusement to the middle generation who wonder how their grandparents could have been so gullible, and a mystery to children.

(5) About the time the employee had finished his spring cleaning, two youngsters hopped up the steps leading to the pit. They stared at the Giant for a minute or two.

"What's that?" the little girl asked.

"The Cardiff Giant," answered the boy, who had read the nearby sign.

"How stupid," said the little girl. And they wandered away.

#

Those special kinds of content must come from reporting. Once at the typewriter it is too late to try for anecdotes, dramatic narrative, and so on. To get descriptive quotes, you must be attentive during interviews to the environment as well as the way things are said. To get dramatic narrative details, you must be on the scene of events, or ask persons who were there to recall for you, word by word, action by action, what happened. To make facts more meaningful, you must seek comparisons, or graphic presentations, or meaningful syntheses. You must be conscious as a reporter of the value of anecdotes and illustrations and ask your sources: "Well, can you give me out of your experiences an example of that?"

When arranging your material for the story, you can do two other things to ease the work. One: <u>categorize</u> your information as much as possible. Two: be sure to have <u>transitions</u> clearly taking the reader from one part to another.

First, categorizing. You might divide your information about a debate over rights of student athletes into these blocks:

(1) The arguments being put up by athletes about their right to long hair.
(2) The counterarguments of coaches.
(3) What the laws, or regulations, say.
(4) What others—students, parents, teachers—say.
(5) The predicted possible outcomes.

Once thought out, outlined, organized, the story is easier to write; it is easier to read. It is logically presented.

You might also present a series of points, then follow up each point in exactly the same order. Like this for a lead:

Anchorage, Alaska—Span the Bering Strait with a bridge to Siberia. Buy Texas. Build fish hatcheries. Hand out $4,000 to each of the 250,000 men, women, and children in this state.

Those are a few of the projects Alaskans are suggesting as solutions to their state's oil windfall exceeding $1 billion. . . .

Confronted by the challenge of simplifying masses of information, depth writers are always telling the reader what to expect 1-2-3 and then telling him the details 1-2-3. Like this:

Black legislator Julian Bond of Georgia makes three points about the American Black's drive for equality:
1. He must keep free of political party alliances.
2. He must encourage "separatism" which other minorities developed in gaining their full share of citizenship.
3. He must be prepared for hard times ahead.

As for transitions— well, that phrase is in itself a transition. Three words only, but they take your attention back to the boldface paragraph on page 100 where you were told a discussion about "categories" and "transitions" was to follow. For the past 800 words you have been reading about "categories," probably having forgotten completely about "transitions." Three words at the beginning of this paragraph refresh your memory and redirect your attention to the new topic.

When writing the long story, you must be conscious of using transitions. When you change from one topic to another, you use a transitional phrase or word. Like these:

In contrast to Mr. Bond's remarks . . .
On the other hand, his opponents say . . .
Still another viewpoint . . .
But . . . Yet . . . However . . .

Sometimes when taking the reader back to a previous subject in your story, you use a "refresher" transition:

In reference to the Black being ready for hard times . . .

About the hard times he had mentioned earlier in the speech, Mr. Bond predicts . . .

Then, used more than any other kind, are the *connecting transitions* that relate one paragraph to its previous one. There are countless time, subject, and place transitions in that category. Merely beginning a paragraph with

Mr. Bond also said . . .

ties it to the previous one. Words such as

Then
Meanwhile
Next
Before
So
Again

at the beginning of a new paragraph are *connectives.*

The best advice for giving a story one last, perfecting reading is this:

1. Reread it aloud to let your ear pick up the rough spots. Rewrite all weak areas.

2. Check all your verbs for exactness of meaning, and change as many "is's" (and other intransitive verbs) as possible to action verbs.

3. Check each paragraph for proper transition.

4. Be sure the lead is interesting and appropriate.

5. Look for dull spots where you can possibly lose the reader and see if you can use ancedote or example or dialogue to bring them alive.

6. When all is perfect, trim the story at least a fifth. Most writing benefits from forced pruning.

7. Give the story to a qualified copy editor for further refinement—and to test it for someone else's response.

Basically, in writing you must see in your mind the pattern of the story. You must work on the lead until it is perfect in getting that pattern under way. You must write with narrative, dialogue, examples, and impressive facts—with the attitude of a short-story writer. You must be able to rework, tear apart, rip asunder, alter, dismember, and put back together your own story until you sense it is perfect. Then you must be willing to subject it to editing by someone else who can see beyond your own ego.

The Case-Study Technique

Another pleasant route for the depth writer to take—*find one person representative of many and tell only his story*. Focus. A central subject. One thread to the narrative. A single pattern to follow. All of these points make the case study tempting.

A reporter and a photographer from *Look* magazine set out to compile a story about "drop-ins," those who come back to school to try again. From the first day of reporting, the *Look* team amassed mountains of statistics, and slag heaps of optimistic quotes from teachers and administrators of vocational schools, and piles of experiences from dozens of students. The material was impenetrable, unmappable, and quite dull. Much of it had been said before. The solution: to find one student whose story represented that of most drop-ins. The *Look* team found the student in California. Here was Focus for the story. Around his comments and experiences—and his feeling of desperation—they could arrange some of the statistics and the quotes from others. The story had pattern. It would be easy to read and follow. And the reader could empathize with another person, whereas it would have been difficult to get excited about a tangle of statistics and disjointed quotes.

(The story of the *Look* team is told in a film distributed by the magazine—"The Unique Advantage.")

The case study, a way of telling a story. And you, the journalist, are the most recent member of a long line of storytellers going back to the minstrel and balladeer. And just as the balladeer, to keep interest in his long long narratives, used the chorus, and the dramatic narrative, and central characters to empathize with, and suspense, and definite style and lilt—well, substantially those same techniques are used by the 20th-century journalist.

SOME OTHER KINDS OF LEADS TO STUDY

Most depth story leads are extended, using several paragraphs to set the point, the mood, and the purpose of the story. (All leads quoted are from *The Wall Street Journal.*)

Such as this lead, which creates mood for a story heavy in *mood:*

NEEDLES, Calif.—It's so hot here, the natives like to say, that residents need overcoats when they go to hell.

That's a tall tale. But it's the kind of story that flourishes naturally here on the broiling Mojave desert. For Needles is one of the hottest towns in the country—and in summer, the living isn't easy.

Almost every day from June through September, temperatures soar over 100, occasionally approaching 122, the record here. Air-conditioners whir around the clock. Radiators boil over. Green lumber curls up in the heat. Pets pass out in overheated cars. Tourists stagger into doctors' offices with heat exhaustion.

A case-study lead:

Orville Pitts says he isn't interested in coming to dinner. He'd just like to work out in the gym and do a little swimming.

He says that's what he had in mind when he applied for membership last spring in Milwaukee's Fraternal Order of Eagles, which has a gym near his office. "I'd gotten a little flabby—I needed a place where I could get back into shape," says the one-time boxer who's now a city alderman.

But his application was rejected; the Eagles say they didn't find him congenial. Mr. Pitts sees it differently. He says he was denied membership solely because he's a Negro, and he's hopping mad about it. Indeed, he's suing the Wisconsin Department of Revenue, which has granted the Eagles a tax exemption. He charges the exemption makes the state party to the alleged discrimination and therefore in violation of the "equal protection" clause of the 14th Amendment.

"The exemption is absurd," fumes the 36-year-old Mr. Pitts. "This means black people are helping pay the taxes of Eagles even though they can't become members."

Wisconsin isn't the only state currently embroiled in litigation over alleged discriminatory practices of private clubs. (Now the body of the story.)

A contrast lead:

HANOVER, N.H.—"Big Greener" or "Creeping Weenie"?

If you're a Dartmouth man, the distinction is crucial. This, remember, is the he-man unit of the Ivy League, where a lumber jacket thrown open to the cold is the uniform and a good time is a skiing junket or an all-out beer bust. Women are sometimes objects that one imports for weekends or travels heroic distances to pursue.

No more. Trauma has come to this campus in the New Hampshire woods, in the form of 70 young ladies undertaking a one-year experiment in coeducation. Undergraduates at other previously all-male schools such as Yale and Princeton have welcomed female students. But a sizable proportion of the more than 3,000 Dartmouth men have decided that they don't want women. Or so they say.

A lead based on an example or an illustration:

RYE, N.Y.—Jerry Rollins, owner of a Sunoco filling station in this wealthy New York City suburb, got riled up recently when a well-to-do local resident handed him a check for $2,759 for gassing her Bentley sedan.

"She was paying 1968's bill in full," he says. "All of a sudden, it hit me. She lives in a monstrous $1 million estate and pays her bills only once a year. I've got a wife and five children to feed and a $23,000 house mortgage eating my gut, yet I have to wait a full year for money she owes me. So I told her, 'No more gas unless you keep your bills current.' "

Thus did Jerry Rollins lose a customer.

Most of the affluent in Rye and around the nation are able to take their time paying their bills. Some occasionally don't pay them at all. Many of the rich build up huge charge accounts and pay no carrying charges on overdue bills, as most middle-class wage earners must. These wealthy persons often ignore bills for months, although credit terms are tightening for most Americans during the current period of tight money. (And now the story is developed.)

To Do, to Read, to Think About

1. For a set of facts gleaned from a new almanac, or a report from community or campus, set the facts into meaningful frames of reference for your readers. Also, set up charts, graphs, other visual forms of presentation.

2. To familiarize yourself with the elements of prose style, refer further to Edith Mirrielees' *Story Writing* (The Viking Press) or books about writing magazine articles by Hayes Jacobs and Frederic A. Birmingham. For more details about anecdotes, first-person reporting, and so on, see *The Student Journalist and Creative Writing* (Richards Rosen Press). Read collections of short stories to get a sense of "Introduction and Development," of Pace in Writing, of maintaining Suspense and Interest . . . just as you should read poetry to develop a sense of power in words and statement.

3. Investigate further the relative strength and weaknesses

of the 5 W's lead and the extended lead. Especially, look for interest factors, one versus the other.

4. Films to see: about the case-study technique, "The Unique Advantage," from *Look* magazine. About reporting in depth, "Did You Hear What I Said?" from The Newspaper Fund, Box 300, Princeton, New Jersey.

FIVE DEPTH STORY IDEAS

When brainstorming ideas, you must be sure to examine the POLITICAL and the GOVERNMENTAL.

1. With what political leaders do students at your school identify; what does this indicate about political trends?

2. What are student attitudes and activism in regard to ——— ——— (some contemporary political issue or problem)?

3. Student government—just how much is it "government" and how much "student?" (Also, you might trace the evolution of student government on your campus—to more and more authority, generally.)

4. What makes some students leaders?

5. Where and who are the real power centers—the decision-making centers—of your school?

Chapter VII

EDITING AND PRODUCING THE STORY

Successful production of a depth story requires team effort. The TEAM. Reporters, editors, photographers and illustrators. A few commercial publications, magazines mostly, have realized that success depends upon close cooperation of that trinity.

The editor is consultant to the reporter, whose work has been discussed almost exclusively to this point in the book. The editor helps evaluate information as it is gathered. He suggests other sources to check. He helps assess the validity of what has been accumulated. He helps plan special techniques: "Looks like we had better go with a case study in this story." And he takes the lead in assigning photographers, cartoonists, and artists to the story. He assumes responsibility for calling in extra reporting help. He takes the lead in reserving a page—or whatever space is needed—in a future issue of the publication. He plans the layout of story and illustrations, in consultation with reporter and photographer.

The editor also sets times for meetings of the team. He settles problems and disagreements. He watches for assignments not completed, and possible news angles overlooked. He may devote great amounts of time to brainstorming the story: "We just plain need a fresh angle in order to make the reader really sit up and take notice of this story." He reports to the editor-in-chief. He may even in commercial newspapers get needed funds for travel budgeted and paid.

The reasons for an editor on the team from the beginning, rather than at the very end, should be obvious. First, the reporter should not be tied down by the multitude of technical and ad-

108

ministrative details that can go into completing a depth story. Weeks may be involved. Second, the story may involve several members of the staff, and one person must coordinate the traffic. The demands of a depth report cannot rob the staff of so much time that the regular edition suffers in quality. Third, a depth report demands special layout techniques or it may appear to be a dull gray mass of unreadable type smudging the publication. To plan for the eventual brightness of layout, the editor must think far ahead of the deadline. Fourth, the editor is supposed to be an experienced journalist who can contribute sound ideas to the team as the report develops—as well as provide a critical eye on its progress.

Of course, one reporter can be given a depth assignment and, if allowed enough time, complete all the stages by himself— from reporting to final layout. But then he would be dropping it as a stranger onto an editor's desk, and chances of successfully processing it into a highly polished printed product would be minimal. Also, there must be either illustration or typographic ingenuity to the layout of the story and that eventually would bring in at least a second person.

Therefore, the best depth reporting develops from the strength of, and the interaction within, a team. Editor. Reporter. Illustrator. And then perhaps additional reporters and other staff members with their special talents. The editor's duties then, in review:

1. Brainstorming; perhaps originating the idea and assignment.
2. Critically reviewing each stage of reporting and writing.
3. Coordinating and advising individuals on the team.
4. Planning layout.
5. Writing headlines; writing captions.
6. Reporting progress to the editor in chief, clearing space, taking care of administrative details within the publication.
7. Selecting photographs and artwork—in conjunction with the illustrators; sizing and cropping illustrations.

8. Providing motivation, inspiration, leadership.

The duties of the reporter have been explained:

1. Reporting the story, perhaps with help from other reporters.
2. Writing the story.
3. Perhaps originating the idea; contributing to the general brainstorming sessions.
4. Working with editor and photographer; making suggestions about layout, picture ideas, etc.

The photographer's duties:

1. Photographing all phases of the story—from getting photos of key persons interviewed to trying to photograph action at events covered as part of the story.
2. Contact-proofing negatives to give to the editor.
3. Consulting with the editor as to what photos to use, how to crop them, how to work them into layout.
4. Making final prints—after decisions have been made from the contact proofs.
5. Providing complete information for captions for the photos.
6. Consulting with the reporter to be sure photographs are coordinated with what is being reported.
7. Helping brainstorm the story as it develops.

The important qualities in an editor are patience and understanding. He edits a story but never heavily rewrites it to fit his own preferences; he works within the framework of what the reporter produces. He makes decisions in consultation with other members of the team, not exclusively by himself. He guides, not directs. He realizes that his is the easiest job; the reporter and the photographer face the difficult challenges of on-spot reporting. The editor must respect their limitations and frustrations. It is one thing to say, "You ought to have gotten that." It is another

Page 8 — The Evanstonian — Oct. 23, 1970

It's a beautiful Homecoming

"We're still No. 1," exclaims the still on the third-place float of the Michael seniors in the festivities beginning Homecoming on Thursday Oct. 9. Although the religious significance of Yom Kippur that weekend created an obstacle, Homecoming got around it by scheduling the football game at 3 o'clock Friday and the dance at 8:30 Saturday evening. In the float contest, Boltwood seniors took first place with a float that one student described as "a box with Willy Wildkit standing on top," Bacon seniors took second.

The Homecoming queen was Linda Jean-Paul, Boltwood senior. Her court consisted of Bonnie Abelman, Beardsley senior, Jill Karwoski, Michael senior, and Penny Summers, Bacon senior. After the parade and the pep rally—featuring the Boltwood kazoo marching band—the Wildkits ran over their opponents, Proviso East, 41-6. The dance Saturday evening ended the festivities. (Photographs on this page by Bob Lieberman.)

DEPTH IN PHOTOGRAPHS. An unusual method of depth reporting is the photographic essay. Such as this full-page of random photos taken during homecoming weekend at Evanston Township High School. Like a depth story, the photographs show several phases of homecoming from several points of view. Instead of a long story or several stories about homecoming—the routine pattern of coverage—Editor Judy Hsia, photographer Bob Lieberman, and the staff decided to let pictures tell the story.

thing to realize it would have taken a miracle to do so. He keeps his team encouraged and inspired. He compliments as well as criticizes. He makes his contributions in positive terms: "I think the story will be greatly improved if you can get back to the board president one more time to ask him for further details." Not: "Go interview him again!"

One of the basic decisions to be made before the story is written: How to package it.

The possibilities are four:

• Break the long story into several shorter parts to be printed in several issues as a series of articles.

• Publish the entire story and all the illustrations at one time in one part of the newspaper or magazine—which usually means a page must be cleared of ads. Jumping the story from page 1 to an inside page usually hurts readership (readers do not make the jump).

• Break the story into several pieces, such as main story with charts, separate anecdotal stories, separate analysis story, a human interest feature as a sidebar, and so on. This is called "packaging the story." The pieces should be displayed together on the same page, however, under separate headlines (see pages 39 and 46).

• Plan a special supplement to the newspaper, maybe a 2-page or 4-page insert in the regular 8-page issue (see Chapter 8).

The "series" idea is weakest. No one has proved that readers eagerly look forward from one chapter to the next. Or that readers when confronted by Part 2 will remember much from Part 1. Usually a series of short articles can be worked into the existing format of the paper without trouble. But impact and readership may drop off. If a series *is* planned, each new part must incorporate somehow a résumé of what has been published.

And each section must be carefully planned to cover just one phase of the whole story. It must be given a set headline (a title, in other words) to identify the series. There must also be a "content" headline. Like this:

Dropouts—the Measure of a School's Failure

Part Two	'You Don't Feel Wanted, So You Don't Stay Around Long'

(*This is the second of a five-part series about dropouts at East High School. In Part I last week* . . .)

At the end of each part must appear a tag line preparing the readers for the next part. Like this:

(Next Week: 'It's tough on the outside, too.')

Generally, special layout techniques will be planned for each part of the series. (Maybe a piece of artwork will be set into each part as visual identification of the series—maybe profile of stumbling student). Maybe each part will be boxed the same way—the entire section enclosed within a 4-point black rule.

Each part should appear on the same page in the same place, preferably on page 1.

Most difficult of all, each part must end on a strong note so that the reader will anticipate what comes next. Like the old-fashioned Saturday afternoon cowboy or adventure serial at the neighborhood theater: the hero left dangling from a cliff.

The series should be advertised an issue ahead of the appearance of Part I, perhaps as a boxed notice like an advertisement on page 1. Perhaps the series can be promoted by posters on bulletin boards.

Finally, unless a paper is printed at least weekly the series will be ineffective. Too much lapse of time between installments.

As for printing the entire story with all its sidebars on a page or two, the inherent problems are these:

● Getting a strong top-of-story headline—across the entire width of the story.

● Working in enough subheads or illustrations to avoid long unbroken columns of type.

● Using plenty of white space around and within the layout.

In the next chapter, several such displays will be reproduced with accompanying critiques.

One excellent idea to be considered: devote one special page in each issue to a story in depth. *The National Observer* does that with the back page. *The Tiger* of Little Rock Central High School, Arkansas, does it usually on page 5 of a 6- or 8-page issue (see page 96). In every issue, in the same place, a full page of reporting in depth.

Some other comments about editing the story:

Put as much information as possible into statistical charts, graphs, tabulations, listings, etc. Long paragraphs of such details in the middle of a story can render it dull, even unreadable. Rather than enumerating in a prose paragraph the parts of a budget, set the budget in some visual form—such as the traditional "pie" with each slice representing a portion of the total budget. The editor should take the lead in this area.

A long list of names would be better set as a sidebar to the main story than included within the story itself.

Maps may help show locations. Symbols from the subject matter—as from the peace movement—could be designed by a staff artist and set into the text to break up the gray.

When many persons must be interviewed, bring in other reporters. Let them track down specifically assigned information and then give it to the principal reporter to be worked into the story. Sometimes a random man-on-campus survey will fit into the story; a team of reporters quickly can get that information.

Do not hesitate to use artwork. Whether cartoons or art illustrations, they work as effectively as photographs in adding new dimensions to the report.

Give by-lines freely. The principal reporters and writers. The photographers and illustrators. An occasional commercial publication even recognizes the editor:

Reported and Written by Henry Smythe
Edited by Jane Magerkurth

Then somewhere within the package photographers and artists are recognized.

Photographs by Stan Snaggle

If the story has strong impact, one of the best of the year, it definitely should go to page 1, even if it takes up most of the page (see page 46). It is happening more often, this giving page 1 to a major story and/or photograph. At the least, on page 1 give prominent display to a "refer" to the depth story if it appears on an inside page.

Are student services really services?	See report on page 5

Two front pages using "refers" to inside stories—from Rincon High School in Tucson, Arizona, and Wisconsin State University, Oshkosh.

To Read, to Do, to Think About

1. In this area of editing and production, you need highly specialized advice. Therefore, these books are highly recommended as guides:

For ideas about makeup techniques and devices: *Modern Newspaper Design,* by Professor Edmund C. Arnold (Harper & Row, 1970, $12.95).

For ideas about selecting and editing photographs: *photograph plus printed word,* by James Magmer (Midway Publishing Company, Birmingham, Michigan, 1970, $4.95). Or, any of several books on yearbook production.

How to fit copy to available space or how to judge how much space copy will fill: *Taking the Fits Out of Copyfitting,* by Professor Glenn Hanson (MulTRul Co., Fort Morgan, Colorado, 1967, $6.95)—with MulTRul included.

About copy editing and the work of the editor: *Modern Newspaper Editing,* by Professors Gene Gilmore and Robert Root (The Glendessary Press, Berkeley, California, 1970, $9.95), or *The Art of Editing,* by Floyd K. Baskette and Jack L. Sissors (Macmillan, 1971).

About writing headlines: *Newspapering,* a guidebook to better student newspapers, by Bill Ward (NSPA, 18 Journalism Bldg., University of Minnesota, Minneapolis; $2.50).

For examples of modern makeup techniques in the student press, see *The Student Press 1971* (Richards Rosen Press, 29 E. 21st Street, New York 10010; $12.50).

Five Depth Story Ideas

Explore the SCIENTIFIC and ENVIRONMENTAL.

1. Is it possible there are persons who are anti anti-pollution—those who see the movement to clean up the environment as being in some way a negative movement?

2. Why have science and mathematics lost their luster in the curriculum in recent years, with humanities perhaps becoming more imperative and more elective among students?

3. How do weather extremes (subzero temperatures, blizzard, 100-degree temperatures) affect the school, the students, the institution? (Reported when one such extreme occurs.)

4. What is student reaction to the latest scientific advancement ——————————— (whatever it is)?

5. Is ecology, as the saying goes, really "man's last fad?"

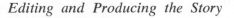

THE TURN OF THE DECADE is examined pictorially here and described in a special report on page 10 of today's Stater.

A page 1 devoted largely to "refers."

POLLUTION AT UF:
Does Any Real Problem Exist?

By GAYLE MCELROY
Alligator Staff Writer

DEPTH REPORT

Billows of burning oil pour from smoke stacks behind the engineering building leave tell-tale ashes on nearby autos. Swirls of oil and surface water are all that remain in a rain-soaked, deserted parking lot. Reports of mud-like sediment filtering through a dorm's faucets are filed in November.

And eye brows are raised, but not very high. For the university looks to the city, and the city turns to the county, the county turns to the state and the state to the federal government. Pollution becomes everyone's problem, yet no one's.

Dr. Roy McCaldin, an air pollution expert in environmental engineering, thinks UF is "relatively a pollution free area," but admittedly has not run tests on campus or in the vicinity.

"Our research is done elsewhere. We work at a power plant on the Gulf Coast and have gone as far as West Virginia and even Arizona to do pollution studies," he said.

While McCaldin was busy doing his research elsewhere, Courland Collier, assistant professor of civil engineering and a Gainesville city commissioner, was delving into local aspects.

"The university and city of Gainesville are the biggest contributors of pollution in Alachua County," he said, listing the causes of contamination.

Automobiles and fumes from stacks behind the engineering building head the campus list. Sulfur dioxide, a major source of "bad air," is emitted from the three smoke stacks, he said.

Sludge in the Gainesville sewage treatment plant, burning at the garbage dump, and an oil backup used to generate electricity during cold weather, have brought complaints of "foul odors" from residents.

The complaints have finally pushed the city commission into action. Something the county did a year ago. Something the state and federal governments did years ago.

In March, 1968, city ordinances prohibiting existing and future sources of water and air pollution were presented to the commission by Dr. Edward Byrne, former public health director, and B.C. Pafford, his assistant.

Both ordinances would authorize the commission to grant exceptions only under stated conditions and require periodic sampling and testing by the city health officer. Neither ordinance has been approved.

The water pollution ordinance would require approval of plans and a certificate to operate sewage disposal systems or waste treatment facilities.

If the air pollution ordinance were in effect, new industries that could cause "bad air" would have to be approved by the commission.

Both ordinances were referred to a special investigative committee. Collier, two representatives of local engineering firms and Director of Public Utilities John Kelly sit on the committee.

Approval of the ordinances are awaiting a solution to the present system of generating electricity in Gainesville. The city is now on an interruptable supply of gas which converts to oil during heavy gas usage in winter months.

Kelly must present a solution to the oil burning, which is a major source of area air pollution.

There are several alternatives, such as buying a higher grade oil, paying a higher rate for gas or burning a cleaner fuel during stable air conditions.

People concerned about pollution are optimistic.

"Kelly said he'd have something in the near future," Collier said.

"I have hopes the city and county ordinances can be sent together to the Florida Air and Water Pollution Control Commission," Pafford said.

Pafford, who is now director of the Alachua County Environmental Health Division, was hoping they both could be sent to Tallahassee this week.

The county ordinances, passed a year ago, may lie in his office waiting state approval a little longer if he waits for approval of the city ordinances.

"No, they won't come up within a week," Kelly said. "Hopefully, they will be brought up within 30 days."

Kelly defends the contaminated areas and his reasons for delay on the new ordinances.

"We burn gas ninety-five per cent of the time. And the five per cent of the time we burn oil, the pollution may or may not exceed the standards set in the new ordinance," he said.

"There are other oil burning places in the city which would be more of a danger," he said. "but I'd rather not pin-point them."

He blamed the delay of action on waiting to review new state standards approved last week.

"Our failure to act at this point was because a majority of our committee felt it would be futile to get local acceptance, but then get turned down at the state level."

But Pafford looks at the state laws in a different light.

"They are often weaker than local laws," he said. "That's the reason we have local laws, so they can be more specific."

Yet he sympathizes with Kelly's delay.

"The problem of burning oil

SMOKESTACKS FROM ENGINEERING BUILDING
... do they cause air pollution on campus?

is an economic one. The city is justified in trying to balance this out. It'll just be a matter of time and they (the ordinances) will be brought before the commission," he said.

Pafford stressed that the ordinances were mostly to keep pollutant-forming industries out of Gainesville and the county.

"They are preventive ordinances and public health is a preventive business. We owe it to the public," he said.

Pafford compared Gainesville to other places.

"We have better air than most places and there are no polluted lakes in the county," he said.

"We have a good water surveillance program and sample every public water supply in the county every 30 days. Several times a year we check all surface areas in the county," Pafford said.

But he admitted, "Some private water supplies are polluted."

Some area pollants are on their way to being eliminated, though.

Complaints of burning refuse at the city dump may soon decrease with the increase of burying refuse in sanitary land fill, said new City Manager Harold Farmer.

"The city has purchased eighty acres of land fill southwest of Gainesville which we might move to," he said. "This is the cheapest way to dispose of garbage."

He explained that the commission recently approved over $1 million for the expansion of the sewage treatment plant.

"I've had some calls about odors from the sewage treatment plant. I suppose this constitutes come type of pollution," Farmer said.

Photos By

Tom Kennedy

POOL OF SLUDGE AND DEBRIS BEHIND ENGINEERING BUILDING NEAR UNION
... experts say there is no real pollution problem in Gainesville.

Chapter VIII

THE DISPLAY

The Single-Page Display—One Story

Put all parts of a report in depth together and they will dominate a page. The problem is to break up the page so that the text will not form a formidable block of gray. For a long report about pollution affecting students at the University of Florida, editors of *The Alligator* used at least five items other than the story to produce a bright, loose, and readable page.

1. A strong, bold headline to top the entire story display, in this case a 42-point, all-caps kicker headline . . .

POLLUTION AT UF:

and a 36-point "content line" under it . . .

Does Any Real Problem Exist?

which also, interestingly enough, provides the topic-line for the depth report. A long story must be supported by a visually bold headline—big, black, innovative, and surrounded by white space.

2. Photographs set into the story, without interfering with

the logical continuity of the story. The text is easy to follow from column to column. The photographs (or you could use artwork) fit into the general characteristic of a depth story—bigness. Captions are kept to a minimum, relying on the story itself to fill in part of the information. For captions, one line of body type, boldface, is set in capitals; a second line is set in upper- and lower-case letters.

3. White space. Lots of it. Headlines surrounded by a framework of white space. Photographs kept separate from adjacent text by white space. Lots of white space between columns of type: Each column is 11 picas wide with 1½ picas of white space as column dividers. The text is set in 9-point type on a 10-point slug, which allows for white space between lines of type. This page could have been set in four columns of type, perhaps, with each column 14 picas wide and with 1½ picas of white space as dividers.

4. Special logotype for identifying the story as a special. "Alligator Depth Report"—distinctively designed and set into the story. Several such "bugs" can be designed to identify and to illustrate long stories.

5. Occasional paragraphs are bold-faced to break up the monotony of type. Subheads would serve the same purpose.

Depth stories generally are displayed on inside pages of the publication. Surrounded by pages of text, they more than ever need careful design.

Incidentally, this kind of report merits an editorial stand on the opinion pages. It should lead to courses of action suggested to readers or to analysis by columnists.

The folio line identifying the page number could have been dropped for less clutter. The reporter's by-line should have been equal in strength with the photographer's.

The Single-Page Display—Page 1 with Related Pages

Editors of *The U-High Midway* (University High School, Chicago) turned to reporting in depth long before it became the

The U-High Midway

Vol. 45, No. 15 ● University High School, 1362 East 59th St., Chicago, Ill. ● Tuesday, May 12, 1970

The school and political stance

Can it even seem to take a position without stifling opinion?

Can an institution take a political stand and still maintain an atmosphere where the viewpoints of all members of the community can be expressed and heard?

This question emerged Thursday when the faculty released a collective antiwar statement (formulated at a meeting Wednesday at which all teachers were not present and not endorsed by all those attending) and Friday when the school was closed because of "the dangerous nature of the present domestic and international situation."

A student faculty committee Thursday had finalized plans for wide ranging war protest programs Friday in which students and teachers could participate if they wished, with school open as usual (story page 2).

IN A MIDWAY interview, Lab Schools Director Francis V. Lloyd Jr., who independently decided the Lab Schools should be closed Friday, explained how and why he reached his decision.

After eight hours of debate Thursday evening, he explained, the University faculty senate with the endorsement of President Edward Levi, decided the University should suspend classes Friday in mourning for four students killed by National Guardsmen earlier in the week during demonstrations (in which most or all of the four evidently were not participants) at Kent (Ohio) State University.

Provost John Wilson telephoned Mr. Lloyd 11:30 p.m Thursday, told him of the University's decision and said the Lab Schools were not bound to it and Mr. Lloyd was free to make his own decision.

"IT REALIZE I was on the other side of the fence during the hora toriums, as far as taking a stand is concerned," Mr. Lloyd said, "but because of the serious and dangerous nature of the present domestic and international situation I felt the Lab Schools should close. The current situation is much more

AT A LUNCHTIME rally Thursday, war protest plans are finalized.

Photo by Mark Friefeld

desperate than the Moratoriums."

Mr. Lloyd said he was aware he might be offending students who disagreed with the school's viewpoint and that students were depending on the use of the school as headquarters for protest activities Friday, but that closing the school was the only way it could officially take a stand as an institution.

Mr. Lloyd said the official reason for the school closing was in mourning for the students killed at Kent.

Before that decision, however, opposition already had been voiced to faculty members making any kind of collective statement.

AT THEIR meeting Wednesday, most of the teachers present signed statements which said, in part, that they joined their "collective voice to that of faculty groups across the country in demanding an immediate halt to our government's most recent escalation of the conflict, as well as the larger war of which it is a part . . . mourn the Kent University students . . . further assert

that such improper use of force has the effect of a campaign to destroy the character we seek for our schools."

The statement on the war was endorsed 87-7, the statement on Kent and repression, 86-7.

Social Studies Teacher Tom Eisemen, in an open letter to the school community distributed after the meeting, declared, "I feel the recent actions taken by the faculty of the Laboratory Schools with regard to the Vietnam War and Kent State violence jeopardize freedom of expression.

"Whether or not the faculties of the Laboratory Schools have acted officially is inconsequential. The fact that resolutions condemning the Vietnam War were passed by the faculty 'collectively' in a meeting called by the Policy Committee in which proponents of the 'collective' argued that the School should take a position on the War' can be perceived by our students as an official act . . .

"IT IS MY opinion that school has an obligation to maintain an atmosphere of political neutrality. 'Collective' judgments on political issues invite the possibility of peer group intimidation. The risk of such intimidation, I believe, outweighs whatever can be gained by petitioning our representatives in Washington Such judgments also intellectually close the door on impartial consideration of opposite viewpoints . . ."

Regarding the closing of the school, Incoming Director Philip Jackson told the Midway Friday he believes the Schools should have remained open.

"High school kids had offices and speakers set up in the school, and the younger Lab Schools kids were too young to know what was going on and thus had nothing to do Friday," he said.

"And you don't call a day of mourning four days after a tragedy," he added. "A day of mourning is the result of shock, as in the assassination of John Kennedy or Dr. Martin Luther King. You don't decide on it four days later."

THE NURSERY School of which Mr. Jackson presently is principal remained open in agreement with Mr. Lloyd.

Incoming Principal Margaret Fallers also said Friday she was displeased that the school was closed.

"Schools should be very cautious in entering politics," she said. "They're the last bastion for independence of thought, where all opinions can be expressed.

"The most important characteristic of a free society," she continued, "is a respect for the views of the minority. If you have a really strong bunch of liberals, the conservatives feel intimidated, they feel inclined to follow the majority views, against their personal beliefs.

"DURING THE faculty meeting, one teacher stood up, said he thought he was misrepresented in the 'collective' faculty petition, and pointed out at least two others were with him, but were hesitant to express their views. That's a heavy cost on the minority.

"The school system should be apart from the political structure,"

she pointed out. "The cost is too heavy if it isn't.

"Could you picture the situation if the school closed in support of Nixon?", she asked, "It's the same principle."

Students who organized war protest activities for Friday said they were initially upset when they found the school had been closed and their original plans ruined but felt their program of gathering signatures on antiwar petitions, letters, and in other programs in the community succeeded nevertheless.

ALTERNATE CENTERS of operation quickly were set up at students' homes.

The students also said they felt it unfair the school should take a stand as an institution.

"We're against the war," said Senior Bob Jaffe, "and are expressing our feeling in our own way, but students who are in favor of Nixon shouldn't be forced to support him With the school open, kids could make a choice, now they can't."

Senior Emily Mann noted, "Both students and faculty voted not to close the school so we could use its facilities and not impose our feelings on others. We felt the protest should be individualized, not institutional policy.

"The decision to take a stand ignored the student and faculty vote, and interfered with our initial plans but, as a project, the entire thing worked out beautifully, maybe better than if we would have had the school."

Special issue

Two pages reporting antiwar activities and related developments at U-High were prepared late Friday night and early Saturday morning for this issue of the Midway by a reporting team of Mark Palmkin, Mark Seidenberg, Barbara Golter and Bruce Goodman and photographers credited under their photos. Because of a crowded print shop schedule, no copy could be set in type after Saturday noon, but an attempt was made to cover protest plans for the coming week. Regular issue content begins on page three.

You CAN Kill the Revolutionaries: But you can't Kill the Revolution!! Remember KENT!

SIGN of the times.

Photo by Mark Friefeld

DIFFERENT KIND of sign.

Photo by Mark Friefeld

popular thing to do in the student press. The reports are of such significance they frequently move to page 1 and then jump to inside pages. Editors asked this question: "Can a school take a political stand and still protect an atmosphere of free debate?"

Students, faculty unite in mass anti-war effort

Why four prefreshmen got suspensions

Events passed SLCC by, outgoing president says

The answer from the report: "No!" The death of four students in May, 1970, at Kent State University provoked the report.

The same five makeup factors were used here as by the staff of *The Florida Alligator* in the example that began this section. Except: instead of boldface paragraphs, here the beginning of some paragraphs are set off by bold-faced and capped words.

Whenever that device is used, editors should ask that a slug of white space be inserted above each such line.

The package coverage of the problem, as well as of the anti-war moratorium of that month, was continued immediately on page 2. To complete the special coverage, the editorial page was devoted mostly to commentary about the war and the politicalization of a school. Editors carefully planned their coverage and layout to coincide.

The Single-Page Display—Several Related Stories

Science Fair led editors of *The John Marshall Rocket* (Rochester, Minnesota) to a report in depth—but instead of by one main story, by several stories about various phases of the fair. Two reporters did a feature story about an unusual student project (Machine Turns Dit-Dot to 'A'). Another reporter spent a month preparing a story in depth about the background to science fairs, both local and national. A staff survey sought answers to why so few students participated in the fair. All items were incorporated into a one-page report planned several issues ahead of time.

Your attention is called to three special makeup techniques. Two stories are set in "double column" type widths. "Only 2% of Students" is set in lines 24 picas wide (first technique) for extra impact and readability. "Report to Teenagers" is set 22 picas wide to allow for a box (no. 2) to be placed around the entire story. Instead of the usual subheads the editors placed "inset heads" such as

**Welte Wants
Bigger Fair**

into the text. The right-hand story was also segmented by the use of asterisks (* * *) and plenty of white space.

Vietnam veterans give some support to the war—But . . .

'It just doesn't seem like self-determination with us over there'

By Geoff Dorran and Kathy Key

Spectrum photos by Mike Graham

Trooper waits in monsoon rain for orders to move out

Bill Kroger

Doug Sherman

Ex-paratrooper tells of war

'How many guys

have we lost

that could have

contributed

to our society?'

The Double-Page Display—Several Related Stories

The problem of traffic regulations and their enforcement was subdivided into several stories and parceled out to staff reporters, photographers, and artists. The results were packaged into the two pages of the centerfold of *The Index* of Oshkosh High School, Wisconsin. However, the layout was not continuous and the separation of the two pages (gutter) interfered with the continuity of the main headline: "Hot-rodding, Stickers Constitute OHS Student Traffic Enforcement Problem" (see page 130).

Two items to note. First, staff artists were brought onto the depth-reporting team. A cartoon plus illustrations under the main headline, both printed in green, dressed the pages. Also, in a listing in the right-hand column, editors ran the license plate numbers of all unregistered cars found in the student parking lot.

The Special Section, Supplement, or Issue

For the 1970 interim elections, the staff of *The Evanstonian* (Evanston Township High School, Illinois) decided to produce a special 4-page insert for their regular weekly newspaper. First of all, a name for the section—INSIDE. Other student newspapers use such names as Probe, Dimension, Perspective. Then special artwork for the nameplate and perhaps a special, boxed item on the first page of the supplement to explain what is being done, how, and why (see page 131).

The rest of the supplement, in this case of four pages, is laid out like any newspaper, although a different headline type might be used, and the page format might be of four columns rather than five. Color helps to mark the supplement with distinctiveness —also more artwork than normal is used.

For INSIDE, editors decided on horizontal display, spreading their stories across the pages, rather than down. A photograph cropped distinctively and sized prominently gives impact to page

Hot-rodding, Stickers Constitute OHS

Councilman Wollangk Explains Lot Procedure

Early in the fall, Student Council initiated the selling of parking permit stickers with the idea that students would have to sign a paper agreeing to the rules of the lot. Their parents would also have to read and agree to the lot privileges based on the conditions set by the Council.

Did you buy one of the 573 parking stickers Student Council sold this year? According to a recent Index survey, drivers of 170 cars did not, and approximately 169 cars were getting by with last year's stickers.

Checks Made

Dick Wollangk and Henry Netzer, senior co-chairmen for Student Council's parking lot committee have run six checks in the lot.

They began putting warnings on cars without stickers, but when that did not seem to be working. "We put signs saying.

Sign Set Up

A larger sign with the rules of the lot set up at the entrance was made. "If the kids see the rules," explained Dick. He also said that probably most of the kids did not realize that a piece of paper they signed in order to get their stickers.

Another possible solution would be more strict enforcement by police of all parking zones around the lot. "we could get all the cars into the lot and get a record of them," concluded Dick.

The Council is attempting to solve the problem concerning the parking lot, but Dick commented, "We don't really know how we're going to enforce it."

OHS Receives Complaints

by Karen Medley

"For a number of years, the percentage of driving accidents and traffic trouble is relatively low," said Mr. Byron Weess, vice-principal.

General View

The general view of the public seems to bypass the problem. One driver termed student drivers as "a myriad of driving problems.

Complaints made that should be directed to any young driver are automatically directed to the public high school, namely OHS, complained Mr. Weess.

"What has that got to do with the speeding 'problem' around the school," said Mr. Weess, "would be pretty hard to follow up, exclaimed Mr. Weess.

Last year the police saw a need for driver education as a result of the road. New stop signs were also installed resulting from another.

Responsible Attitude

"Traffic is everyone's concern," concluded Mr. Weess. "All are in-

Mr. Michael McGinley

Minority Creates Problems, States Drivers Ed. Instructor

by Nancy Lambrecht

"I see about 20 thoughtless, reckless drivers in the school parking lot — a small minority not belonging to OHS," stated Mr. Michael McGinley, head of OHS's driver education department.

"Most do a good job but most of the time," he continued. "There is a problem, but it is caused by a few who must be stopped," he stated.

"The driver education teachers do a fine job, but there is the young son from applying for his license," Mr. McGinley continued, "if two too early to tell if there was any improvement since the law was passed in 1967.

The issue was then raised that if the driving age were raised, or not raised to 40, whether or not there would still be a need for driver education.

"Same problem," Mr. McGinley stated, but he also said it might be a bit less of a concern because of driver behavior and human behavior are inseparable.

"The driver is the primary cause of most accidents," the in-

structor stated, after indicating that driver education was made a requirement for getting a license if the applicant is under 18. He also added that it was too early to tell if there was any improvement since the law was passed in 1967.

Hot-rodding Endangers Everyone

Hot-rodding or speeding is a problem around OHS, according to students and homeowners.

A recent random sampling of persons in the high school area showed that speeding causes accidents, playing in their own yards. It is difficult for pedestrians to cross the street, and the noise from the cars disturbs classes and annoys homeowners.

more chance of accidents." "Senior Carol Gunther said, "Speeding is going to happen wherever you are, in the street or in the high school area here is nothing unusual."

A woman homeowner commented that speeding causes children from playing in their own yards. Last year a little boy was riding on the hood and it flew onto the school lawn. It would have been dangerous if he would have hit someone who "horn-way around" on top of a motor

principal at OHS.

The high school gets its share of complaints, admitted Mr. Weess and some of these are up-

Survey Reveals Lack Of Concern Toward Stickers

Three surveys taken by representatives of the journalism class showed that 24% of driving students at OHS were parking without a sticker in the high school lot.

On Nov. 4, 20% of the cars in the lot didn't have stickers visible.

A second survey on Nov. 6 showed 22% without stickers, while a third survey on Nov. 26 indicated 29% of the cars, minus the football-shaped sticker.

Listed below are the license plate numbers of the cars and students without a sticker.

Student Traffic Enforcement Problem

Editorial

Don't Have An OHS Parking Sticker? Neither Do 169 Other Students

Is your parking sticker? You don't have one??? Well, neither do 169 other student drivers at OHS, according to a recent Index survey.

So, B8119, you really don't need one. As far as anyone can see, there is absolutely no need for having a parking sticker. The Student Council is unable to bar anyone from use of the lot whether or not they have a parking sticker or not.

And what if you had purchased one? Well, your name, license number, and a description of your car would be on file in the office.

What will happen to you then when you don't have a sticker? Probably nothing. The Student Council seems to have the backing of neither the OHS administration nor the student body (witness the Oshkosh High School Blue Book).

"Forbid Student Use Of Car" Suggests One City Bus Driver

A rule forbidding students to take the city bus was one of many solutions offered to the hot-rodding problems by city bus driver Jacob Kaufmann expressed the views of many of his co-workers when he said, "The greatest percentage of student drivers are all right, but there are some who spoil it for everyone."

Mental Midgets

Others did not bother to differentiate. One driver termed students as "mental midgets."

Commenting on the actual hot-rodding, bus driver Patrick Mayed joked, "It's a good sport if you make it." On the serious side, Mr. Kaufmann said, "Students who drive in a reckless manner do not realize the danger of death to themselves or others. They just think it's fun."

Stricter Licensing

"I think a stricter licensing procedure would help many of the problem drivers. This, of course, must apply to the young not the

rules are made in the OHS official rule book.

So what do these professional drivers think of OHS hot-rodders? Mr. Patrick Mayed exclaimed with a shudder, "I DON'T think of them!"

Mr. Robert Koenigel stated there would be no business given to students until they are 18 or out of high school.

"Boot" Aids Enforcement

A possible solution to the parking problem is the "Auto Immobilizer" or the "boot," manufactured by the Rhino Products Corporation of Eugene, Oregon. It has been successful in controlling parking regulations at several universities and places throughout the United States.

The immobilizer fits over the front tire's wheel, so the car cannot be moved.

According to Rhino Products officials, a special wrench is the only tool available that can remove the boot.

Eugene, Ore. used the immobilizer to catch two persons who had accumulated 100 unpaid tickets. The first victim had 29 unpaid tickets, and the second victim

call from the police may begin to patrol the lot.

In the administration, dial 231-5151 and post $2.00 tickets on 169 drivers and R8119.

All articles and research done on the OHS parking lot and hot-rodding problem are from Mr. Ron Harrell's fifth hour journalism class.

Contributing members include Pierre Bierly, Brian Brooks, Sharon Falk, Pam Freiburg, Nancy Lambrecht, Karen Medley, Roy Goss, Vicky Middle, Sue Sostag and John Behrendt.

pay their fines.

The price of the immobilizer (plus wrench, 100 notices, mailing antics and instructions) is $69.95. An extra bolt is $9.95, and an extra wrench is $14.95.

Oct. 30, 1970 — The Evanstonian — Page 3

INSIDE THE Evanstonian

EVANSTON TOWNSHIP HIGH SCHOOL · EVANSTON, ILL.

Political caucuses work in elections, moratorium

by Jennie Berkson
and Cathy Cambal

No matter how many times you've heard it, it's not true; ETHS is not an island. Through the Political Union, a newly formed organization, concerned students involve themselves outside the school in community and national affairs. Several of the individual caucuses within the union have organized outside activities which support certain candidates and beliefs.

Currently the Democratic caucus is canvassing for Senatorial candidate Adlai Stevenson III and Congressional candidate Edward Warman. Some members are now working at Stevenson's Evanston post. They are aiding other workers by mailing literature and telephoning citizens. On election day they will be urging people to vote and tabulating election returns.

"The best way to make your point of view heard in this country is to work within the system by supporting candidates who are closest to your point of view, instead of being anti-everything and ending up not being heard at all," Mark Alger, chairman of the Democratic caucus, said.

According to Mark, the students will work with Operation Breadbasket after November 3 elections.

In contrast, the Republican Caucus is campaigning for incumbent Representative Phillip Crane, who spoke at ETHS last Monday.

The caucus is planning to have a representative of its party come to ETHS to set up a Young Republicans of Evanston Club. "The Republican party is trying to redefine American goals and ideals," said Apu Ghosh, head of the Republican caucus.

Presently, the Independent Voters of Illinois Caucus is involved in precinct work which includes supporting IVI candidates. Among the candidates are Senatorial Candidate Adlai Stevenson, Congressional Candidate Edward Warman, State Treasurer Candidate Benjamin Kucharski, and incumbent President of the Cook County Board, George Dunne.

According to chairman John Throop, the group is currently canvassing for Stevenson and Warman.

Last Tuesday, the IVI sponsored guest speaker Dr. Michael Bakalis, democratic candidate for State Superintendent of Public Instruction. He spoke at the Illinois Education Association meeting to interested students and faculty.

Unlike the other caucuses, the students for Israel have made the elections a secondary issue. According to Gary Paul, SFI chairman, the purpose of SFI is to involve Jewish students in Jewish political activities.

One recent activity of the SFI was to organize a large turnout for the Soviet Jewry rally last Saturday at the Civic Center. Debbie Matek, alternate chairman, stated that further plans will include speakers from Habonim and

Hashomer Hatzair, both Zionist youth groups.

Like the SFI, the Radical Left Caucus has placed the elections into a secondary position. The caucus is more concerned with tomorrow's Moratorium at factories and shopping centers. According to Tony the leaflet includes information on the use of tax money which goes to Vietnam among other places.

The Radical Left's other plans include proposed guest speakers such as Eva Jefferson, Northwestern Univ. student body president, and Marilyn Marcus, Student Mobilization Committee representative.

Although the Radical Left Caucus is not strictly an antiwar group, the members do participate in the SMC meetings and do support many of their ideals. "Despite Nixon's so-called peace propositions, there is nothing new in his policies," Tony remarked.

The Radical Left Caucus is not the only caucus working for the Moratorium. Several caucuses of the Political Union and many other organizations not specifically affiliated with ETHS are taking part in it. Among the activities for the day are speakers, skits and a march beginning at 1 p.m. at State and Wacker and proceeding to Grant Park.

Mr. Harry Wood, sponsor of the Political Union, summed up the political union. "The success or failure of this Union rests upon the students, for they can determine its future by how much effort they put forth."

Campaigning for Adlai Stevenson III Michael junior Mark Alger distributes some literature to north Evanston resident.

In local elections
What is the level of student body awareness?

by Adelaide Whitehouse

Students and teachers alike don't seem to agree on whether students are politically aware and/or active.

"Some students are aware politically, but even fewer are active. More kids are aware of national rather than local elections and I would like to see more students active at the local level," said Miss Barbara Dean, Michael history teacher. "I suppose the non-interest could be justified by the fact that high school students can't vote yet," she said.

Mr. Carl Hammer, Michael CS teacher, disagreed with Miss. Dean. "You can tell kids are more aware just by how much they talk about political issues," he said. "Some students in my classes are precinct captains for the canvassing of Adlai Stevenson.

"I do think students are beginning to realize that issues

can also be won at local levels. For instance, the petitions were circulated in order to get merchants to stop selling detergents high in phosphates," said Mr. Hammer.

"When I was in high school we weren't as politically oriented as students are today. I identified more with national figures until college when I beacme more politically aware," he said.

Michael junior Bill Randall felt students were apathetic to politics in general. "I think students are more concerned with social affairs. Students are more aware, but not necessarily more active, because of the mass media and daily school emphasis on politics."

Michael senior Carlos Figueredo, who is originally from Cuba and has been living in the U.S. for two years, sheds some light on another aspect of political a-

wareness that no one else mentioned. "Students in America take an interest in what's going on in their country, and if they think something is wrong, then they try to change it," he said.

"You can't do that in Cuba because it is a dictatorship there and that has a lot to do with the reason you can't dissent. I think too many students take their right to dissent for granted, and that's why more students aren't more politically active," Carlos said.

One student expressed his confusion with trying to understand elections. "I don't consider myself politically aware or active, but I do try to hear both sides of whatever the issue is," said by John Starr, Beardsley junior. "The trouble is, many times both sides are right," he said.

"I think most students are politically aware, but that they can't succeed when they are

active because of the great difference of opinion in the school and the country," John continued.

"I think students are definitely more aware today than even ten years ago, " said Mr. Harry Wood, Bacon political science teacher. "In my regular classes we discuss political issues as long as it's relevant. In my advanced classes you can't keep away from discussing politics because it is an integral part of political science," said Mr. Wood.

Ann Dunlop, Michael senior, disagrees with Mr. Wood but cites a different reason for lack of political activity on the local level.

"Students aren't aware or active on the local level as they are on the national level. The reason for this is probably because there is no attempt by the local government to inform students about what is going on to get students

active," said Ann. "It's up to the school or parents to inform the students as to what is going on."

Mr. Alan Mumbrue, Boltwood history teacher, offered a hopeful note for students like Ann who feel that someone is responsible to keep students informed about political issues.

"All of my classes are definitely aware of the political system and issues because that is what we are currently studying," he said. "I think it's indicative that the elections are very much on the students' minds by the articles they bring into class to discuss."

Are students politically aware and/or active? To some extent every student is politically aware simply because of political promotion and advertising. As Ollie Killheffer, Bacon freshman, put it, "Commercials make me more aware of the election and its issues."

1. Headlines are bigger than used normally—on page 1, a top head of 42 points, then one of 36 points and bold-faced. The result is a strong, streamlined appearance.

In organizing the "book," editorial comment went to page 2, a student survey to page 4. The supplement was inserted into the usual 4-page weekly of October 30, 1970.

The Recurring Depth Section

Artwork, imaginative reporting angles, and strong headline work brighten the "Perspective" sections of *The Daily Kent Stater,* Kent State University, Ohio. Typical is this 4-page reportage of the women's liberation movement on that campus.

Artwork usually shares attention on page 1 with the main story. Sometimes graphs or charts or free-hand illustrations add visual impact.

In this issue, for subheads impact-statements are extracted from the stories, set in 12-point type and broken into the body text (see lower right, page 1). The name of the section, "Perspective," is specially designed.

To keep inside pages of the section alive, illustrations are used profusely. Stories are displayed horizontally. A variety of inset subheads are used as on page 3. Sometimes page 2 and 3 are laid out as a single unit (see pages 134, 135).

"Perspective" explores in depth, with packaging techniques, such issues as Veterans on Campus, Suicide among Students, Politics during Election Year.

FIVE DEPTH STORY IDEAS

Look for the PERSONAL and the MORAL.
1. Among the generations what are the differing meanings and levels of "taste," "responsibility," "working within the system," "conformity and individuality," "obscenity," "getting out and working for a living?"

Women's Liberation at KSU

Members explain
attitudes and goals

By Doreen Sapir and Mary O'Neill
Perspective Editors

"I have been interested in women's lib ever since I found out there was a name for some of the feelings I had."

This thought expressed by art and psychology student Barb Taylor, echoes the sentiments of eight Kent State women interviewed for **Perspective** to find out what the campus movement is all about.

Their organization would eventually benefit both males and females, they explained. From the time you are born, you are taught how to react in a given situation. Men are told not to cry, while females are told that crying is a part of femininity. This is just one example of society's standards.

"Society's attitude has often trapped males in an undesirable role also," a member said. The interior decorator or the clothing designer

Perspective

During the interview, members commented that theirs "is not a movement that can be defined in 25 words or less." The movement, to members, is more a way of approaching persons as individuals, rather than in the masculine or feminine roles assigned to them by society.

They regard these "traditionally binding" roles as the key factor in their oppression as females.

Elaine Wellin, a graduate assistant in sociology, recalled that she and some friends became involved with women's liberation about three or four years ago.

"I now know I never really got involved then, though," she commented. "Later on, it hit me at a more personal level, and I realized its importance."

Val Boaz, a psychology major, related an incident from the Columbia riots that demonstrated the point that even the "radical" males didn't understand what Women's Liberation was all about:

Following the militant student takeover of the administration building, she said in an exasperated tone, the men turned to the group and ordered the women to fix them something to eat. They were really shocked when the women indignantly refused.

are two male roles that are often unjustifiably viewed as effeminate.

Men are also denied the opportunity to express themselves through tears or deep-felt emotions. If they allow their natural emotions to become visible in public, they are looked upon with disgust or as emotionally unbalanced.

These "standards" are what liberation is trying to get rid of. What we want, commented one member, is the right to be ourselves without being judged according to sex roles.

Monica Whelan, an art major, commented, "In my life there exists a certain vague dissatisfaction with filling the woman's expected, preplanned role of the domestic."

Sally Weaver explained that she shared this feeling.

"For a long time I thought that this dissatisfaction was something wrong within me," she said. "But I found that that wasn't true; it's not something wrong with me, but with the society that I was raised in which tells me that my role is in the home and nowhere else."

During World War II, they pointed out, women were expected to leave their homes and fill the positions vacated by men. They did so — and they did so effectively. But then after the war they were supposed to readjust and be satisfied once again solely with their role in the home.

'Society's attitude has often trapped
males in an undesirable role also'

We are a group of women dedicated to learning who we are and what liberation is, explained one of the members. We're not a group trying to prostitute the word "liberation."

Part of their philosophy is that no one is bound to a set of rigid organizational standards. Each of us is at a different level of liberation, a member commented. We cannot present ourselves as a group with a solidified set of ideals, because we are still each seeking our own individual identity.

"Even the word 'organization' implies a power structure that just isn't there," commented Miss Wellin.

With 51 per cent of the world population being female, ours is a movement that would affect the entire world, commented another member.

Everything from magazines to situation comedies reflected this attitude. Women were depicted as not having the intelligence or emotional stability to handle jobs requiring a high degree of intellect or stamina.

For years, someone explained, women decried the pollution of the air and water by industries. Rachel Carson's book, **The Silent Spring**, first illuminated this issue. But now that ecology is a nationally recognized problem, men have taken over the position of spokesmen and are ignoring the women who first recognized the problem, she said.

This is the type of attitude and action that the movement is trying to expose and alter, the members said. Equality and individuality — that's what KSU women's lib group wants, they agreed.

Wednesday, November 25, 1970

P - 1

Survey indicates support
Is there a need for a day care center?

By James Shultz
Campus Editor

Students, faculty and non-academic employees are responding with interest by showing the need for a university-sponsored day care center, according to a survey coordinator.

At the end of the present quarter, the survey will be presented to Richard E. Dunn, vice president for business, as a suggestion to be implemented in planning.

The survey, circulating as a petition, says that "one of the top priorities for university budgeting" should be day care centers and a cooperative nursery. At the present time, top priority in the 1971-72 budget is a new gym.

PERSPECTIVE STAFF: editors Donna Sapp and Mary O'Neill; staff writers Dennis Trueloos, Eric Johnson, Sid Marville, Karen Lombardi, Jeann Schulte, Lou Godefroy, Kris Winslewski; cartoonist Chuck Ayers.

mented, the suggested that education majors could work with children and psychologists could do studies.

A day care center for children of students recently was approved in Kent for about 25 children at capacity.

"The need is obviously much more than, for 25 children, every one of whom have children, too."

"It is unfair to women to be denied an education by a society because they have children," according to a student from the area, a mathematics professor and survey coordinator.

"Likewise children should not be penalized by inadequate care because their mother is not conscientiously at home," she said.

The day care center supporters contend that a good number of the university community should be able to use the facility. According to them, such care should be basic, just as the Health Center is for students.

Organization for the survey is being led by departments, according to the survey coordinator, who will have the responsibility to collect all forms and turn them in.

"We are not asking for a special program for the branches," said Mrs. Dykes. She said the group wants anything that would prove most adequate.

Mrs. Landers said adequate facilities would include trained personnel. The university could gain advantages from the center, Mrs. Dykes com-

KSU staff differ on whether pants are 'in' the office

By Linda Lombardi
Staff Reporter

Who decides what women must wear at the office?

"Orders come directly from private," relates one secretary. "Each department has jurisdiction over the dress codes," according to another secretary, and yet another young office worker said the job at hand puts it up to one's own judgement.

Phoebe E. Price, assistant to the vice president for research, in Lowell Office, each department may set their own dress standards. A student at the other extreme, "I'd never wear slacks. I'm written down or anything, but the first day I started work here, I was told to wear a skirt or equivalent."

Then came the varied responses by women who stated that some office, on campus to discover just how women feel in regard to the branch. Various stated how they feel quite the same way.

The first pants suit found its way into the Division of University Branches House last week and was met with various comments and male administrators and female members of the staff.

Richard O. Coates, coordinator of special programs for the branches, had to agree with his colleagues. "I don't really give them a choice in the office or in pants. I have no objection though, because they do look neat and dressy. However, I personally prefer to see a woman in a skirt."

Paul I. Fisher stood alone among the men when he said, "I think they (pant suits) are very appropriate for the office." Fisher is coordinator of purchasing at the branch office.

Other women in the office tended to take sides with Fisher. "I think slacks are attractive and as practical if we made. I'm wearing it, Esther Moyer secretary.

Another secretary added, "I love them. It sure beats looking at underwear."

Ed Heverick, student employee, commented as he sat working in his blue jean bells, "they make me neat and they should be worn because they're more comfortable."

This attitude evoked various other comments upon visiting offices.

The secretary at Data Processing got the extreme, "No, when confronted with the pant suit question."

"The directors of our department have decided that pant suits are not proper dress for the office," she said.

It's unfortunate, Payable and Payroll Departments, Payable and Payroll Departments all of the 14 secretaries. When asked if she wouldn't wear a pant suit to work, the secretary exclaimed, "Sure, if I had one!" And the typist in a 44 inch cast!

Another commented that "the men down the hall all wear pant suits!"

Mrs. Margaret Brown, secretary, school of journalism, said that she wouldn't be in favor of wearing pant suits to the office. "I don't think slacks are very businesslike," she said.

At the College of Education, most women had positive attitudes towards slacks in place of the proper dress for the office," she said. "I wouldn't wear a pant suit for a girl filling in the bottom drawer of a filing cabinet to have on slacks (for obvious reasons)."

Dr. J. Keith Vasey, assistant dean in the College of Education, gave his unofficial permission to add as much to the totality of collegiate dress as possible.

Another administrator, Dr. Edward Clark, of the education offices may wear pant suits.

For instance, in the task 1960's, males in the Geology department, said, "I feel pant suits are fine."

The range of clothing styles for coeds today is apparently quite "liberated."

— Stater photo by Dixon McLain.

Coeds curfew 'protection' disappears as Kent State becomes 'liberated'

By Karen Bickerstaff
Staff Reporter

In the past, dormitory life and campus traditions seemed to go hand in hand when it came to strict curfew and visitation policy for women.

This trend has been rapidly changing, however, as the women on this campus have gained no-hours and increased visitation privileges for themselves in the last two years.

The typical Kent State coed of 1970 might not be such a rarity compared to what she was enrolled in KSU during the 1920's.

Back then, girls were prohibited from leaving the campus proper after 6:30 p.m. on Mondays and Wednesdays. Moreover, they were forbidden to leave dormitories after 7:30 p.m.

Lights were expected to be out at 10:10 p.m. on weeknights and 10:30 p.m. on weekends, unless there was a social function one was attending. A girl had to obtain special permission from the housemother to get in any later to study for an exam.

Each morning at 9, except Saturday and Sunday, the girls and studies had to be ready for inspection.

After curfew hours

Lights out 10:10 p.m. 1920 rules

A pamphlet of the period says that all students will be expected to be entertained in the parlors until 9:30 from the housemother in each day, and 10 Friday and Saturday nights.

For automobile riding, another regulated area, was restricted to the 50 miles except in cars. *Our Youth* by Phillip Shriever, "No coed should be out of the city campus without permission of the housemother, and she must be accompanied by some member of the company the couple." In the case two phone calls to a residence hall serve as the extra person for the quarter.

It is, perhaps, quite ironic to note in Shriever's book that "as these students in the early days of Kent had the right to assign 'campuses.' Such a privilege was not something an individual could have taken for granted in the student protest era of the 1970's.

Rules relax following war's end

They were formulated by the Associated Women Students (AWS), with the AWS saying that it had established judiciary functions, regulations and programs to add as much to the totality of collegiate experience as possible.

According to the "Kent Coed" guide for 1969-70, a minimum criteria. If a coed had reached the accepted standards of good behavior, the smoking on the campus or on the streets, for that matter.

10:30 p.m. Monday through Thursday, and by 12:30 a.m. Friday and Saturday nights, except when one is in-beed when it came to strict curfew and visitation policy for women.

If a girl expected to come in after the doors had already closed, she could obtain special permission allowing her to stay out past the usual curfew. The number of 'late per' depended upon the student's class rank. A freshman had four per week; a senior had 12.

No more than one late permission per week. Late permissions may not be taken outside of the residence hall, and on campus, into class or office buildings.

In this newer publication, females were reminded against "wearing socks, instead of hose, to Sunday dinner and using language which is unbecoming to a lady."

It added, "We are proud of the fact that the Kent coed wears blue jeans, slacks or bermuda shorts only in the dining halls only at breakfast and all day Saturday. Women wearing shorts should not go on the front campus, into class or office buildings which is unbecoming to a lady."

To do so, she had to get a written parental statement of consent and not be on academic or social probation.

The total elimination of curfew hours for all women was not far off, however. On Nov. 7, 1969, more than 125 coeds from Beall, Korb and Allyn Halls protested the hours system and the right of the university to impose such hours.

They felt the curfews in effect were "discriminatory" and a "violation of their constitutional rights."

Each girl who took part faced discipline from her dorm. Standards board. All were placed on conduct probation, and all decided to take their appeal to the university. They were represented in their appeal by the Student Bar Association.

Ralph Marshall, assistant director of the Student Conduct Program, sided with the girls, saying "By imposing hours on coeds, the university is actually pushing girls to cheat and lie by staying out later."

He added, "The 18-year-old male student at this university does not have problems with hours. Since he is more mature, but actually the 18-year-old freshman girl, who has hours, is more mature."

Curfew hours end after mass protest

Dr. David A. Ambler, dean of Residence Halls, offered an explanation from the administrative conduct. "Curfews were set up for the health and safety of the students, and for the purpose of an educational climate. No one thought the girls were in danger in the residence halls, but the girls were considered to try to locate their daughter."

Partial plan for no-hours in 1968

Sunday through Thursday, and 2 a.m. Friday and Saturday. If a girl failed to check in her time limit and had not contacted the residence director within an hour of closing, the director would notify her parents and consult them on procedures to try to locate their daughter.

According to the "Kent Coed" booklet for 1968-69, the accepted standards of good behavior, "smoking on the campus or on the streets, for that matter.

Certain halls had a "no-hours" policy. If a coed had met the minimum criteria. If a coed reached the accepted standards of good behavior, she "should" promote a more mature attitude on campus.

But the court also labeled the law's historic anachronism. "They recommended that constitutional review and policy—and take action."

Thus, at the request of various student groups, and despite the curfew, the Student Affairs Council recommended the rules change for all women living in residence halls.

High Court ruled that the curfew was constitutional, and not discriminatory on the basis of sex. The 49 girls were found guilty and given suspended sentences.

Since September 1969, it has been the policy of the university to allow no-hours "should promote a more mature attitude on campus.

P. 3

Wednesday, November 25, 1970   THE DAILY KENT STATER

From a masculine viewpoint

Reporter finds male support for female liberation move

By Dennis Trauben
Perspective Staff

Talk of "the liberated woman" seems to have grown a lot louder. The topic of women's liberation is no longer relegated to just women, but it also has begun to engulf the male as well.

The great majority of males interviewed were in agreement with, or supported the women's liberation movement.

The questions put to those interviewed related their views on equal job opportunities for woman, child day care centers, the role of marriage and family, and whether as males they felt threatened by the movement.

All of those interviewed were in agreement with the statement that women are discriminated against in the area of job opportunities. The answers to the other questions drew various responses or no answers at all.

Dr. Thomas Lough of the sociology and anthropology department felt that the struggle for women's liberation is a struggle for women "to be equal as human beings."

Dr. Lough stated that "most of the women I know in the movement don't want to be equal to the man in the man's world. They want to be treated as human beings, they want to find humanity. They don't want the male role or the traditional female role."

Dr. Lough spoke favorably for the idea of child day care centers run by the community for the benefit of working women who have children.

The liberation movement is also tied into the problem of population control, according to Dr. Lough.

"If the movement (women's liberation) does not succeed we will have a population catastrophe," said Dr. Lough.

The associate professor of sociology said that the liberated women would begin to fill maintenance and service roles such as doctors, lawyers and other types of roles which serve mankind.

Dr. Lough said he feels that women have been trained to relate as if they are behind a mask. He asserted women have been made susceptible to a market of items created to make them look nice because that is what society expects.

"Women succeed not because of what they are, but because of what they look like," Dr. Lough said.

He added that women spend a lot more on wardrobes than men in order to please the male.

"I think it is great," said Thomas Dubis, a history instructor, "women's liberation is as fundamental to change in society as the black struggle for equality."

Dubis said that he views the liberation movement as a struggle for equal social status.

Dubis, who said he is hoping to participate in a free university course winter quarter dealing with "Male Liberation - Men Against Cool," feels that "males are ignorant of a central happening in a woman's life, pregnancy, and its pain, and they fail to give females the due coming to them for their functions in society."

Sophomore Jim Fetters said, "Women should be equal to men...they should be allowed to use their talents as they exist."

"I think it is a good thing, women are suppressed — especially economically," said senior math major Pete Dolfive.

"The stereotype of the female housewife should go out," continued Dolfive, "women should become more individual, but people should be cautious not to emphasize the basic physical differences between sexes."

Business major Mark Bram said, "Women must maintain their dignity and not just be housewives; a woman is an individual with valuable ideas that should be shared on an equal basis."

John Stark, an English instructor, said that he approved of the movement, but that he felt that there are more important struggles to be fought before all our resources are channeled into women's liberation.

"It is so hard to get reform — it is too hard to wage war on too many fronts at once," Stark said.

Burr Editor Harvie Ruffman and student Jerry Brodsky said they were in favor of the liberation of women, but that they should be ready to accept the responsibilities of their liberation.

Journalism instructor Jerry Hilliard said that he felt many women do have legitimate gripes regarding job discrimination, especially after they have received the appropriate training.

Stater Night Editor George Markell, who is married, stated, "I am all for it."

Maybe men are starting to talk more seriously about liberating their partners in life.

An M.C.P. is . . .

"You male chauvinist pig" are words which are flung through the air at a rapid clip by many women's liberation people.

What is an m.c.p.? According to Webster, a male is "opposed to female, strong. Vigorous, courageous;" chauvinist is "a person unreasonably devoted to his own race, sex, etc." and is "contemptuous of others of opposite sex."

Webster says a pig is "a domesticated animal with a long broad snout and a thick fat body." A pig is also regarded as acting or looking like a pig, greedy or filthy."

To summarize, an m.c.p. is a strong, greedy, filthy man who is contemptuous of females.

P - 4

And the women said . . .

By Kathy Wisniewski
Staff Reporter

For the majority of females on the KSU campus, women's liberation presents a challenge — abolishing sex discrimination, particularly in jobs and pay scales.

When asked how they felt about women's lib, most KSU women interviewed by the Stater saw merit in the movement and could identify with it in some way.

"I'm effective when any adult human being is deprived of dignity and is made to play a subordinate role," Miss Nancy Conn, instructor of sociology, said.

"Many women have been socialized to play a child's part. Women's lib may not be a perfect social movement but it does represent the efforts of our largest minority group to achieve dignity and to implement its potentialities as human beings," she added.

"It is absolutely imperative that every woman should get involved in the movement," Jackie Stewart, administrative assistant to the dean of the Honors College said. "It's not a radical-extremist movement — everybody has something to gain by it.

"I don't think I need a man to dominate me. My relationship with a man, if it is to be successful, must be on an equal level.

"Motherhood is excellent but it's not my only goal in life."

According to JoAnn Manzeo, a 22-year-old art major, "Whatever a guy can do, so can a girl, just as long as she keeps her feminine role.

"A woman should be free," Miss Manzeo said, "and if I were smaller-cheated, I'd go bra-less."

"Women are completely equal," Susie Staggers, a 22-year-old graduate said. "I think it's silly that the male is supposed to support the female — they should be on equal terms."

Most of the women agreed that the main frustration faced by today's woman is sex discrimination in jobs.

"I have a job and am supervisor over eight men that are older than I," Karen Lee, a senior business and education major explained. "Although I'm qualified for the job, the fact that I'm a woman makes them resent my authority.

"Women have been dominated for so long that for them to break away is a challenge in itself. The movement has been started so let's go through with it."

According to Sue Brashear, senior speech and hearing therapy major, women have "one legitimate gripe. If a man and woman are equally qualified for a job, there should be no sex or pay discrimination.

Sports is another area in which women are often discriminated against.

"A woman's team doesn't have the same prestige as a man's," Michelle Sandrey, a junior physical education major, said.

Although we put in just as much hard work, we don't get credit for being on a sports team, but a guy does."

Some women are a little leery about the liberation movement. "It depends what goes along with the liberation," Joyce Fritz, a freshman sociology major said.

"If it brings equal job opportunities fine — but I still want to keep my femininity."

"The whole movement is conducive to the basic things a woman wants," Kathy Kline, a senior elementary education major said. "A woman wants affection, deserves respect for her, but doesn't want actual equality. She wants a man to be above her."

Debbie Heck, a junior majoring in social work, would like to see the women of KSU better organized. "The movement could really be effective but I don't think it's organized enough on this campus," she said.

"The way for women to get power is through an organization. It can get rid of abortion laws and salary discrimination. The only need should be made known more."

Perhaps one issue in women's lib was offered by Jean Haraway, an English professor. "I've always had liberation because I've never let anyone take it away from me," Miss Haraway explained. "A man should stand up for what he believes and so should a woman."

THE DAILY KENT STATER

---

2. What are the personal goals of students and how do they compare to the heritage of Goals and Drives that they are expected, by many persons, to conform to without questioning? For instance: the work-ethic . . . being a productive person . . . earning your own way.

3. How much is the school responsible for moral education; that is, inculcating in students a reverence and obedience to an already-defined code of conduct? Several polls of parents as to what they expect of the school indicate they want, first of all, "discipline."

4. What is the relationship—new and traditional—between students and the church?

5. As present students look ahead to what will be history, what image of themselves do they want to see reflected?

A Memorandum from the Managing Editor
of The New York Times

From A. M. Rosenthal, September, 1969 (reprinted in part):

. . . But more and more we have to give something considerably in addition to spot news. We have learned that news is not simply what people say and do, but what they think, what motivates them, their styles of living, the movements, trends and forces acting upon society and on a man's life.

. . . Law reporting used to be simply what went on in the courtroom. We still report that, but we know that we must also report on the relationship of law to politics, law to civil rights, law to labor, law to poverty, the difference between law in the courtroom and law in the squadroom.

. . . In education reporting it is not enough to write about the business of education—teachers, unions, taxes—but of the process of education. What is being taught in the classrooms and by whom? How has the teaching of history, sociology, economics changed? Why? The relationship between student and teacher is a whole new field of news.

One of the most exciting and fruitful areas of news coverage now is the consumer movement, closely allied to the awakening of the importance of the physical environment. In essence, this deals with the impact of a modern, technological society on the individual—what he pays, the value received, the air he breathes and water he drinks—and what he does about it.

To maintain objectivity in an increasingly complicated world demands more knowledge, more sophistication, and these in turn demand more investigation.

. . . And, in the past year particularly, we have rebuilt and expanded our national staff. The United States is probably the poorest covered country in the world, and we hope we are changing that, bringing the feeling of the country into the paper.

Chapter IX

OTHER KINDS OF REPORTING IN DEPTH

There are several terms about kinds of reporting:

Analysis of the news—"What the news means"
Backgrounding the news
Interpretive reporting
Investigative reporting
The follow-up story
Depth story

Often the terms are used interchangeably. Yet each term does signify a distinctive phase of reporting.

Backgrounding—Telling the reader about the events or series of circumstances that have led to a current situation in the news. If a proposal for changing tuition fees has reached the voting stage, then a "backgrounder" would review the series of fee increases in recent years, when the present proposal was introduced and by whom for what reasons, the various steps from that proposal to this vote and the arguments that developed en route. A background story provides a lesson in history. The supposition is that the reader forgets much of what is reported week by week, and at important moments of news he needs a review of what has happened.

Interpretation—A news report is complicated for readers to understand—such as redistricting the school, or merging several schools into a consolidated district. The facts are not enough for understanding. They must be explained to the layman-reader in his language. Explanation, history, definition of terms. Perhaps, an assessment of the significance of the news to the reader.

Causes and effects. All this goes into an interpretative story which, of course, must be written by a reporter who has carefully covered the story.

Tax stories are difficult to understand. It is the reporter's challenge to explain how much a new millage rate costs the taxpayer in terms he can understand, what the terms mean, where costs have gone up and necessitated tax increases, and so on.

Analysis stories are largely synonymous with interpretive stories. Unless you want to make a distinction that analysis can be done only by a columnist or specialized reporter (a Washington correspondent, for example) under his well-known and respected by-line. Then you would define an interpretive story as less complex and written by any reporter, well known or not. All reporters would be capable of some kinds of *interpretive* reporting; only the experts, such as James Reston, would be capable of *analysis*. Analysis might involve more personal opinion; certainly more obvious points of view and conclusions.

Investigation—In this situation a newspaper probes a controversial area in which there is some question of illegality or malfeasance, say, of office. Usually, the reporter documents allegations of misdeeds or corruption. He needs witnessed statements, documents, and other kinds of legal evidence to substantiate the story, much as a lawyer documents a criminal case. This area is highly specialized and very few reporters are trained to be investigators. Ralph Nader is unquestionably the most famous investigative reporter today, even though his work is not part of journalism. *Life* magazine maintains a special investigative team that searches politics and government for corruption.

All four terms are similar in that they attempt to explain the unknown, or the unfamiliar, or the confusing to the reader.

All of these stories would be used along with straight news stories to report the most recent news.

(The shades of difference among various kinds of stories was explained a few years ago by the longtime and peppery editor of the Sunday *New York Times,* Lester Markel. He explained:

(What Mr. Khrushchev says about Mr. Kennedy is spot news.
(Why Mr. Khrushchev says these things is interpretation.
(Whether Mr. Khrushchev should have said these things and what we should do about them is opinion.)

For many years the admonition was to put interpretive stories on the editorial/opinion pages to separate them from so-called objective news reporting. Fine—except that knowledgeable and thorough interpretive reporting is not exactly personal opinion. It is reliable information, based on expert evaluation, presented without bias. It answers the most important question of why?, which puts it in somewhat different realm from those stories that answer merely who?, what?, when?, and where?

Today, interpretive stories are found in the news columns as part of the customary news coverage. These stories are identified by special headlines, such as by this kicker:

Analysis of the News

New Philosophy: Students Pay
More of Costs of Education

Or a boxed headline can be set into the story to identify interpretation:

> **An Analysis
> of the News**

> **What
> the news
> means!**

In fact, the analysis or interpretive story can be used in conjunction with the straight news story, like this:

Board Increases Tuition 33 Percent

What the news means

Students expected to pay more of costs of education

Thus, the story of interpretation is placed *where* readers most immediately will be asking themselves, "What's really behind this tuition increase? Why an increase?"

Investigative reporting is too difficult for most reporters. First, the reporter must know all about rules of evidence; what he documents must be strong enough to stand up in court. He must know how to work with documents and records where he finds most of his evidence. He must know how to persuade persons to reveal sensitive information and stand behind it.

Despite its infrequency, investigative reporting has provoked most of the exposures of severe political and public-servant corruption in this century. Rarely does government police itself, usually only when reform groups or investigative reporters force it to. A Pulitzer Prize went to the *St. Petersburg Times* in 1964 for uncovering fraudulent spending of public funds by some members of the Florida Turnpike Authority. The report took the time of six writers and photographers who worked in five cities. The series of reports filled 4,800 column-inches in the *Times*.

For the *Louisville Times*, reporter Dick Berger went to prison to write about the need for penal reforms. For the Rockford, Illinois, *Register-Republic*, reporter Rodney Wenz got employment as a psychiatric aide to investigate possible reforms in in- stitutions for mentally retarded. A *Newsday* investigation led to five indictments in Florida and Arizona for land-by-mail frauds. An investigation by the *Cleveland Plain-Dealer* led to the con- viction of a county recorder. Another newspaper broke a story about the son of a judge who had been freed by three fellow judges after auto accidents resulting in the deaths of five persons.

From the exposure and downfall of the corrupt Boss Tweed to the present investigations of Ralph Nader, journalists have consistently turned up more cases of corruption and graft than any other agency—including government and police.

Which says a great deal about the power of the press, its im- portance to the individual citizen, and its role of protecting citi- zen-readers.

In the press, controversy is a good thing if it means the reader is being served, and society is being protected.

A group of investigative writers known historically as The Muckrakers at the turn of the 20th century proved the impor- tance and the honesty of investigative reporting. Upton Sinclair wrote a violently controversial novel, *The Jungle,* in which he tried to show how predatory industry had destroyed whole fami- lies of immigrants. Industry, governmental officials, and some citizens attacked him heatedly for the novel. But it was true, Sin- clair protested. *"The Jungle* is as authoritative as if it were a statistical compilation," Sinclair claimed. He had been to Pack- ingtown to live with the people. A special commission appointed by the President verified all that was in the novel.

(Investigative reporters, despite all the initial protest and coun- tercharges of "Lie!," have been proved right in almost all cases. The reports stand up to scrutiny and counterinvestigation.)

One systematic way of backgrounding an issue is the Question- and-Answer format. When the draft system was changed to a lottery in 1969, the Associated Press used the pattern to explain fully its implications. Like this:

Here are answers to some of the more frequently asked questions about the Selective System lottery:

Q—Why is President Nixon changing the draft? The old method wasn't perfect but at least most people understood it.

A—Under the previous method men were drafted between the ages of 19 and 26, the oldest first. It kept a person wondering for up to seven years whether—and when—he might be drafted. Nixon wants to reduce that "agony of suspense."

and so on.

The Follow-up Story

News events move through several time periods.

Advance Story—information about a coming event.

Spot News Story—information about the event printed as soon as possible after the event occurs.

Continuing Story—one of a series of stories covering an event as it takes place over a period of time, following, for instance, the progress over two or three months of an important motion through Student Government.

Follow-up Story—after the event has ended and a considerable period of time has elapsed, a "looking back" at it.

Let's use an example: Student Government in December finally passes a new Dress Code. It goes into effect immediately. Resolution made; debate over; votes in; decision conclusive; regulations in effect. But the story has not really been ended.

In April, editors become interested in how effective the code has been:

How many violations; what penalties?

Opinions now of students and faculty about the effectiveness of the code?

If the new code has in any way influenced Council or school to pursue other changes in traditions?

If any debate still exists on campus about the new code—good, bad, or otherwise?

Any weaknesses observed—with perhaps the Council re-examining the change?

And so on.

All of this goes into a follow-up story of ANALYSIS or EVALUATION. Once a spot story or a continuing story has come to an end, an editor or beat reporter should mark in his Future Book (of ideas) for next week, or next month, or next year a note to follow up the story.

In this LONG-TERM follow-up, *the persons involved* in the original event might be sources for a story. The group in Council who fought the Dress Code revisions, four months later could be interviewed:

Do you still oppose the revisions, now that they have been tried?

Have you changed your clothes style and appearance to abide by the code?

Are you still campaigning for a return to the old code? Do you plan specific measures in Council?

Another kind of follow-up is SHORT-TERM. As soon as the event is over, the reporter may write *a cause-and-effect story* about it. The new Dress Code has been approved. The reporter then tries to project what will happen in the next few months.

Impossibility of enforcement—according to a vice-principal.

Complete breakdown in neatness and modesty in dress—according to conservative teachers. Also, breakdown in discipline.

Colorful student body so bright and varied in their plumage that school suddenly will become interesting—according to liberal teachers.

Past changes by Council have ended disastrously; this one too, probably.

The change brings school in step with campuses across the country (some case studies) that are liberalizing codes to give students greater freedom of movement and idea.

Another SHORT-TERM idea for follow-up. Once the event is over, *the reporter may go back and recall the total history of the event.* The dress code revisions were first proposed three years ago, when present seniors were sophomores. He may recall for the reader the transition from extreme opposition by the majority of teachers and students to now, one of majority approval.

The follow-up story may be *a feature, too.* A story missed during the spot news coverage. Once the event is over, the re- porter's recollections, usually humorous and anecdotal in nature, may provide a story.

There is also the possibility of *historical recall,* the time story. Partway through basketball season, a sports writer decides to do a recall feature about the championship team of 10 years ago. In a sense, all time features are part of follow-up coverage.

Lastly, follow-up may be necessary to provide final facts about spot news stories. *The National Observer,* a weekly newspaper published in Washington, D.C., periodically publishes a column called FOLLOW-UP, a collection of such unfinished news. For instance: a spot news story out of Vietnam claimed that Vietcong forces involved in a desperate charge on American positions were under the influence of drugs. However, the story was based upon suspicion—it was too early for establishing proof. This kind of story is marked by *The National Observer* for follow-up, when enough time has elapsed to establish proof. Two months later, the story—no proof found to substantiate the claim.

Too many stories are left incomplete, with claims unverified, with information left at the stage of supposition. Editors and beat reporters periodically should review previous issues of the paper to search out incomplete news.

Daily newspapers with Sunday editions frequently use one other kind of follow-up story. From Monday through Friday, a series of stories will cover City Council trying to vote upon a new traffic system of one-way streets. For the Sunday edition, the same reporter may write a *comprehensive story* about the entire Council action—with analysis and interpretation included and a map showing the redirected street traffic.

To Do, to Read, to Think About

1. Look at the most recent issue of the student newspaper and for each straight news story ask, "Why?" How many of the stories need some kind of analysis and interpretation; how many, backgrounding? Compile a list of "Why's" to be answered about your school and the student body?

2. Read books by such interpretive and investigative reporters as Howard James, Kitty Hanson, Clark Mohlenhoff, Harrison Salisbury, Sandy Smith, William Bradford Huie, Norman Miller, in some instances Nicholas von Hoffman, T. H. White, Erwin Knoll, Jules Witcover, Malcolm Browne, David Halberstam, Michael Dorman. The best investigative reporting today is being done for *Life* magazine. Among others: *The Nation, Harper's, The New Republic*. You certainly should read the several published investigative reports by Ralph Nader: *The Chemical Feast, Vanishing Air, Sowing the Wind, Dry Water*—all available in paperback from Grossmann Publishers.

Also, be sure to look into the frequent special reports distributed by the government and available from Superintendent of Documents, Washington, D.C. (ask to be put on the mailing list for announcements).

Among commentators and analysts eminently worth reading: William Buckley, James Reston, Vermont Royster, Tom Wicker, Marquis Childs, Joseph Kraft, Arthur Krock (all available in collections, too).

Historically, see Lincoln Steffens, Jacob Riis, and collected volumes from the works of The Muckrakers.

Also see John Hohenberg's *The New Front Page* (Columbia University Press) for details about investigative reporting moving strongly into the news columns.

For further guidance about commentary and editorials, see *The Student Journalist and Editorial Leadership* and *The Student Journalist and Writing Editorials*. For guidance to campaigns and crusades see *The Student Journalist and Thinking Editorials*.

FIVE DEPTH STORY IDEAS

1. Investigate the following:

a. School dropouts . . . or fadeouts (college withdrawals) . . . or drop-ins (those who come back for a second try).

b. Are student services (book store, cafeteria, and so on) really services to the student? Or are they purely profit-making systems?

2. Background the following (historical background or chronology of events leading up to present circumstance):

a. New development, or changes, in the curriculum.

b. The game for a championship.

3. Interpret or analyze the following (who is affected and how? why necessary?):

a. A new school or student council or board of education ruling or regulation.

b. A new technique in education—such as modular scheduling.

4. Explain and define the following (what is meant to the reader):

a. A new dress code or standard of discipline.

b. A new fad or fashion.

5. Personally experience the following:

a. A Day with ——————— (for instance, school bus driver).

b. The First ——————— (day of school, snowfall, protest of year, etc.).

BACKGROUNDING THE NEWS—A STORY TO STUDY

The issue of length of male hairstyles assumed symbolic proportions in 1969 and 1970. Court decisions were handed down —some in appellate court affirming student rights to determine their own hairstyles; some in lower court affirming the rights of schools to assess and to enforce restrictions. One such controversial decision in Texas was backgrounded carefully in the outstanding student news magazine, *The Anvil,* at Memorial High School in Houston. The case was reviewed in its entirety. Readers may have read about it in bits and pieces of stories over a period of time, but never in one cohesive, orderly presentation. What had been disjointed may for the first time have become a coordinated whole in this "backgrounder" by student reporters Mike Shearn and Nancye Hinckley.

Who Measures Styles?

By Mike Shearn and Nancye Hinckley

"Oh say can you see, my eyes if you can, then my hair's too short!" Hair, hair, hair—the new symbol of freedom, individuality, sexiness, and student-establishment "disagreements."

The opening phrase is from a song called "Hair," from the now famous Broadway play of the same name, where hair is a new freedom symbol.

Hugh H. Davis, a "not-attending" student at McCallum Senior High School in Austin, represents the fourth new hairy symbol —students vs. administration-type establishment conflict. Why is Hugh not attending classes? His hair was too long, according to the McCallum principal.

After several debates the principal told Hugh to go home and not return before getting an "acceptable haircut." Hugh and his mother appealed to the superintendent of schools, who told them the principal's decision must be abided by.

In his plight to keep his locks, Hugh and mother filed an injunction against the Austin Independent School District and the principal to allow the student to return to school regardless of hair style.

Counsel for Hugh claimed in court, October 4, 1968, in the 53rd District, that the principal had denied the student of his individual rights by refusing him entrance to school because of his hair length.

Counsel also claimed:

● Hugh had worn his hair this way last year without incident.
● Hugh had no disciplinary problems.
● Hugh was passing all school work.
● The administration had no legal right to suspend Hugh.

The principal had not given specific instructions concerning the length of an "acceptable" haircut.

Long hair worn by students in school causes taunting, which results in disruption of order in hallways and on school grounds, counsel for the school district cited and further added:

● Long hair worn by students at school is an administration problem which goes beyond individual rights.
● Administrative policy, not Board policy, deems extreme hair styles as inappropriate.
● The superintendent and principal have the right to make rules and regulations necessary to the operation of public schools.

After hearing both sides of the case, presiding Judge Herman Jones ruled:

"The Constitution and laws of this state and nation have as one of their high purposes to safeguard the individuality, and diversity, and the right of protest and dissent of each citizen.

"When an individual, in the exercise of his claimed rights, interferes with, disturbs or disrupts the legitimate pursuits of others, organized society must blow the whistle.

"Society, acting through its legally authorized school officials, has determined that certain standards of appearance should be maintained in the classrooms of public schools to promote teaching and learning."

Judge Jones continued, "It should be remembered that this young man is not required to trim his hair. But if he wishes to participate in the educational benefits afforded at McCallum High School, he shall trim his hair and comply with all valid regulations of that school."

School rules and regulations involved in the case were not arbitrary or unreasonable, and therefore did not deprive Hugh of his Constitutional and legal rights, Judge Jones maintained.

Hugh's appeal time has expired. Hugh must either try to enter another school elsewhere, or cut his hair and return to McCallum.

ANALYSIS OF THE NEWS—A STORY TO STUDY

After a decade of growth, expansion, progress and optimism, colleges and school systems were rudely shoved into reverse in the early 1970's. Higher tuition. Severe budget cuts. No-votes on bond issues. Moratorium on new faculty, new equipment. Limits to enrollment. And regression and pessimism became the keywords to education.

When the cutbacks struck hard in 1970 and 1971, college students, for instance, were dumbfounded. A great many had to quit school because they no longer could afford it. "What happened?" they asked. "Why this, suddenly," they wondered. That is when a student reporter-editor at one campus, Jim Landers (a Vietnam veteran), decided an analysis story was needed.

From talking to a number of administrators and legislators for several months as part of his news beat, he had reached several conclusions. None could be attributed directly to any one person; they were cumulative impressions. No official had made any attempt at a calculated analysis of the situation. In fact, officials would rather the problem were kept out of the news. Therefore, from the expertise of long-time reporting and because of the absence of official explanation, Landers decided to write his own *analysis*. Cause-and-effect . . . causal factors . . . here is why the campus finds itself in financial difficulties . . . the substance of an analysis story.

And, perhaps for the first time, the students/readers would understand the situation.

It Starts at the Top

There is a feeling among this University's administrators that the recent budget reductions (winter, 1971) in higher education were not for solely economic reasons.

During the winter quarter, five high ranking administrators expressed, in private, a fear that the reductions are a "backlash" to 1970's student violence. They believe the leading figure in the effort to make Illinois universities "toe the line" is Gov. Richard B. Ogilvie.

In a recent budget statement, Gov. Ogilvie declared, "Universities will show a deficit before I'll let the state budget show a deficit." Adding to the universities' woes is a 1968 campaign pledge by Ogilvie to build $488 million of new roads. The governor and State Board of Higher Education (SBHE) trimmed a total of $414 million from the higher education budget (February, 1971) for 1971–72.

In other years, the universities could seek restoration of funds through the state legislature. But, times have changed. Chancellor John S. Rendleman's budget task force, whose members have visited Springfield almost weekly since early January, has found individual legislators reluctant to defend the universities.

The proposed Illinois budget for the next fiscal year provides for increases in all areas except higher education which was reduced by 22 per cent. According to Gov. Ogilvie and the Bureau of the Budget, the Illinois budget is the maximum possible amount due to the current economic slump. Therefore, if higher education funds are increased and fitted into an already tight state budget, taxes would have to be increased—or other areas cut back.

And the legislators cannot be expected to increase taxes to support universities. Politicians and SIUE administrators agree that the general public mood is anti-college at this time.

The recent revelations concerning the $1,025,000 in federal funds spent on the Mississippi River Festival, the supposed fleet of SIU aircraft, and last year's University House scandal at Carbondale have tarnished the image of the university's fiscal responsibility.

These recent developments plus the memory of last year's campus disorders have created an image of irresponsibility and wastefulness.

The end result of the current higher education financial crisis could mean a wiser, less frivolous use of appropriations in the coming years.

And increased tuition costs with less return in the classroom for the money.

#

"The function of truth is to bring to light the hidden facts, to set them into relation with each other, and make a picture of reality on which man can act."

—Columnist Walter Lippmann,
Author, "Public Opinion," 1922

Chapter X

STORIES FROM ISSUES AND PROBLEMS

Revelation Now.

The name of a new, self-styled "National High School Journalism Review" is symbolic of the student of the 1970's. It represents the NOW generation—those who refuse to wait several years for changes to be made. REVELATION—the pervasive philosophy of students that theirs is a mission to mankind. If it is not divinely inspired, then certainly it is a natural rights mission much as Ralph Waldo Emerson, the transcendentalist, felt it.

Revelation Now. A National High School Journalism Review, Vol. 1, No. 1, October, 1969. Published out of Roanoke, Virginia. Edited out of Cincinnati, Ohio. Edited out of Chicago, Illinois, out of Minneapolis, Minnesota. Edited by high school student journalists with all-American names like Brueggeman (Tom), Neuberger (Steve), Rohrer (Stu), Hamburg (Vicki), Patinkin (Mark), Glassner (Barry), Peoples (Curt).

It was born, in the Fall, of optimism and a compulsion to communicate ideas. If it had a theme, it is what Emerson himself expressed a hundred-plus years ago:

He who would gather immortal palms must not be hindered by the name of goodness, but must explore if it be goodness. Nothing is at last sacred but the integrity of your own mind.

Some of the editors, a few of the contributors, and some well-wishers stood in an informal semicircle in the lobby of the Palmer House in Chicago, in late November, talking about *Revelation*

153

Now. Stu Rohrer of Cincinnati tried to explain the origins of the monthly journal. The seed was planted during the Northwestern University summer workshop for high school editors, he said. Most of the staff first met there. The idea came from a speaker, Henry deZutter of *The Chicago Journalism Review*. In talking about that magazine, an outlet for professional newsmen who want to write about journalism, he set *Revelation Now* in motion.

Final plans grew out of a meeting in a car in Cincinnati, when school started, between Barry Glassner of Roanoke and Rohrer.

(*"The school press has the potential of being one of the great driving forces in this nation," said the first editorial in the first issue. "It is one of the most highly read mediums to which high school students come into contact. If high school journalists do not work together to make their newspapers vehicles for improving this nation, we have not fulfilled our responsibilities as journalists."*)

Despite discouraging odds of getting sufficient circulation and enough capital, high school seniors, who were already editing school newspapers, found still more time, more reserves for another paper.

It may come as a surprise to professional editors and publishers to hear that high school students call themselves "journalists" and with pride. But these students have been raised in an Age of Information, *the* Age of Communication. So young, and yet the need for honesty and morality in journalism has been driven in deeply.

Stu Rohrer explained the economics of the first issue: 66 students contributed $3 each to get it under way. The press run: 2,000 copies. Stu and Curt Peoples edited it in Cincinnati; Barry took care of printing and circulation in Roanoke. It then was cast across the country; and fingers were crossed.

("It is time for high school journalists to be free to publish relevant material," the first editorial continued, "so long as they conform to journalistic standards. At present, high school journalists are censored by three groups: 1) principal or administration, 2) parents, 3) advisers. None of these groups belongs to the newspaper's intended readership.")

The traffic in the corridor of the Palmer House was heavy, and a number of people turned to look with curiosity at the 10 or 12 students clustered enthusiastically, talking about a mutual project. Not every person would agree with the premise for *Revelation Now,* the students said. People had been skeptical, one of the students allowed; and there had been a couple of instances of negative attitudes openly expressed. Stu Rohrer said, however, that all in all the response to that point had been positive.

("The antique theory that high school newspapers should publish only news occurring within the immediate confines of the school can no longer be substantiated. Students are being called upon by adult leaders for involvement in political campaigns, city and state improvements, reformation of the draft system, changes in the church and numerous other out-of-school areas. Their ability to handle these responsibilities will come from their knowledge of the subjects.")

The important thing about *Revelation Now,* and the agreement was unanimous: "We do it completely ourselves." The person interviewing the editors had expressed amazement at the excellent makeup; why weren't their own school papers so smart in appearance?

Uncomfortable shifting of feet. Some tentative starts to comment, then the thinking better of it. Finally, "Well, we do it completely ourselves. No outside interference."

"Does that mean you're saying no one is looking over your shoulders?"

More shifting and reluctance. "Well, we're just free to do whatever we want to do."

"You mean you have no advice from a professional?"

"No, we do it ourselves."

Well, in all of American history, the spirit of doing it yourself has been prevalent. "Do your own thing!" the students say. The Bible says:

> In those days there was no king in Israel; every man did that which was right in his own eyes.
>
> (Judges XXI, 24).

The westward migration was spurred, in part, by the desire for self-reliance, for independence. The whole of transcendentalism— Henry Thoreau and Ralph Waldo Emerson and Bronson Alcott —is taught with a kind of reverence, even fervor, in high schools, and it, too, is based upon the integrity of the individual's soul, spirit, and mind.

But there was a slightly uneasy shifting and reluctance to speak because students were doing their own thing. Perhaps they felt the possibility of disapproval if they admitted it too firmly.

> (*The first editorial was frank, however: "It is when the established high school press is not permitted to discuss topics of controversy that the underground newspapers are formed. . . . The underground press is, then, a rebellion against the established press. Like most acts of rebellion, the writing tends to be emotional. It seldom employs good journalistic practices."*)

The interviewer was persistent. Trained much too long on negative news values, he asked a little more pointedly: "Are you part of the underground press?"

The unanimous agreement: "No." All were staff members of bona fide, establishment-recognized, aboveground, official, few-issues-confiscated, legitimate, student newspapers. This was their second dedication—considered just as bona fide, aboveground, legitimate, and student-centered.

(*That first editorial answered the question: "The founders of* Revelation Now *feel there is another alternative. We believe that by working together on techniques for handling important issues and problems, high school journalism can grow up."*)

"Can grow up!" They were eager to talk, these editors 16, 17, 18 years old. Top of the class in high school. Destined for Ivy League, Big 10, the Northwesterns, Columbias, Antiochs, Harvards. Most planning futures in communications. Their journalism already unusually slick. Mark Patinkin of Chicago went down to Skid Row to do a Christmas story about, "For him this is no season to be jolly." There was Tom Brueggeman, of the *Evanstonian* of Evanston Township High School, which had a year before declared itself free and independent of bulletin-board items and henceforth concerned only about what is important.

To the interviewer—not so fresh from 15 years of teaching—the enthusiasm was pleasantly contagious. There is a new lifestyle here, born of affluence, better education, television, and for the first time since the factory system encroached on human rights, a belief in, not rhetoric for, the American philosophy. The hair is long, but groomed carefully to ear-level, collar-level, eyebrow-level. Mustaches—a godsend to the teenage male whose problem has always been lack of lines of expression or other signs of character in the face. Nehru collar, low-rise slacks with a flare at the bottom, unconsciously flicking hair out of eyes. Twenty-five years ago, in the school paper, we were concerned mostly about a lively gossip column, detailed coverage of sports, and some bulletin-board news about plays or concerts. That was the extent of our intellectual activity—and the depth of our journalistic concern.

(So high school journalism must grow up. The first editorial concluded with this statement. "This publication will contain discussions of practices used by high school journalists throughout the United States. Articles will be published so that newspapers in other parts of the nation may carry them. Revelation Now will be the forum for making high school newspapers relative to the modern student." End of thesis.)

Ironically, these student journalists had been encouraged toward declaring independence and honesty of intentions by underground newspapers in their schools. The subject of "relevance" or "significance" had not often been raised in high schools until the late 1960's when other, nonjournalist students began to take advantage of cheap, instant publication to produce counter-newspapers. A flurry of manifestos. Then the aboveground journalist-student found himself called to accounts for better performance. And student sympathy was not always with the established newspaper.

The underground newspapers were not always kind to the established journal in school:

> As the day starts off, I read another informative issue of our school newspaper. Wow! It's almost as good as the last one. The issue in which Dr. Brauer approves the plan for a new addition to the school. Now for the groovy articles, in the new edition, they really turn me on. It has an All-Star cast of articles, such as "Student Council Lists Representatives," which was a very true article as told by the title.

The school newspaper found itself getting the same abrasive attention from the underground as did homerooms, study halls, hall passes, dress codes, and teachers who showed racist attitudes.

> Oh, we can express our complaints in the school newspaper— but the principal says what gets printed and don't embarrass

the school's reputation. . . . The issues which directly affect us are ignored by established press and "official" high school papers . . .

Thus out of negative comment came the imperative to established editors to change the nature and direction and attitudes and contents of their own newspapers.

For instance, *Revelation Now* in its first two issues declared that marijuana laws were too stringent. There was a story about youth communes and detailed coverage about anti-Vietnam moratoriums. A look back to the youth-centered demonstrations at the Democratic National Convention in Chicago in the summer of 1968. Arlo Guthrie and "Alice's Restaurant"—as a protest against police attitudes toward youth and against the draft. About new movie codes. The draft. Much about Vietnam. And outspoken political commentary:

> Spiro Agnew and George Wallace would have made a great team. Spiro's "effete corps of impudent snobs" (which liberal students took deeply personally) would certainly have complemented Wallace's "pseudo-intellectuals."

A review of Frederick Wiseman's critical documentary "High School." Movies: "Medium Cool" . . . "Easy Rider" . . . "Midnight Cowboy." The New Left, and the New Right. The rights of fellow Black students. And a long story with a banner headline, announcing to all other editors:

> **Evanston Township High's "Evanstonian"**
> **achieves complete freedom of press.**

In many high school newspapers in the country, those subjects could not have been broached. Too controversial. Too untraditional. Too opposed to the ingrained life-style of the older generation. A new life-style. A return to pre-Civil War American values. An outspoken youngest generation. A jolt to long-established mores and moralities.

"Well," said Stu Rohrer, finally, from the loose semicircle of somewhat uncomfortable students, "we're just free to do whatever we want to do."

Plans for the future were ambitious, the students said. *Revelation Now* started as a review of the high school press strictly for editors, but it might turn to a more general purpose. From Minneapolis, the rotating editorship was to go to Los Angeles and Kansas City and New York. Somehow, the mechanics of processing had to be speeded up. A printer had been found in Virginia who did a good job inexpensively. Money was extremely short. Subscriptions were slow coming in. The future was tentative, to say the least—and every professional publisher knows that feeling.

At the Palmer House in late November, the students were busily trying to recruit contributors and subscribers among about 1,700 delegates to the annual convention of the National Scholastic Press Association. They were the center of omnipresent discussions about the positions of issues and problems in news coverage in the high schools. Up to five years ago, at such conventions, the recurring questions from students during formal and informal sessions were these:

Makeup—"How can we make our paper better?"
(An unsettling question—the desire to improve the package but not to worry about the content.)

Gossip columns—"Students seem to like them so why shouldn't we have them?"

"How can we cover clubs and activities so they are more interesting?"

"What is a feature story—we just can't seem to understand the difference between that and a straight news story?"

Most of the questions then were inspired by what was a rather mechanical approach to scholastic journalism, inspired in part by tradition, and in part by most journalism textbooks, which are traditional and often rather paternalistic in attitudes toward what high school students can and should do—and what the system will allow them to do. (Editorialize, yes, but on tolerated topics such as school spirit—an example of the System managing debate and dissent.)

But at the convention in Chicago that fall, there was ringing in the ears of many of the editors this challenge from an underground paper:

> The high school newspaper is a supplement to the loudspeaker or the daily announcements. It gives news of the school. It is not and never will be a forum for ideas and a showcase for creations. The actual reason for a school newspaper is not known; the excuse for it is tradition. "There have always been school newspapers so each school should have one." There is no harm done by school newspapers, so to advocate their elimination is destructive criticism. But the idea that these newspapers have no greater purpose is constructive criticism (deep concern). . . . A lack of communication between generations has often been declared, but an ever larger gap exists among the students themselves. . . . A medium is needed for expression of thoughts and creation.

In hearing that challenge and proceeding to meet it, *Revelation Now* was not exactly the pathmaker. Here and there, across the nation, individual high school papers had issued a new credo. An adviser here, recognizing his function as guide and also as buffer to outside control, had encouraged ideas and intellectuality and imagination. Administrators there who see education as being also ideas and experimentation—and occasional failures—had encouraged a newspaper centered on issues and problems. Students in several places, recognizing they have *some* power, had asserted initiative in revising news concepts and approaches.

The U-High Midway at University High School in Chicago has been far out in front. It tackles every in-school problem with a depth story (integration, teachers' unionization, restrictive disciplinary procedures). It leads in translating national and regional issues to local effects (Chicago conspiracy trial, the McCarthy campaign, voting at 18, the national Presidential elections). It has opened two full pages in each issue to a Forum—to stimulate dialogues among students and faculty.

The Evanstonian at Evanston, Illinois, Township High School one fall nailed its theses on the door of the school system. The editors in issue #1 of the year asserted openly they had room only, from that point on, for news that *vitally* concerned students. No room for routine.

Suddenly, a young staff and adviser at Nashville's Overton High School brilliantly explored school and community problems and changes with depth coverage, packaged in 2-page sections. Religion. The War. Poverty. Those areas and others have come up for scrutiny. Reactions among administrators, faculty, students, and staff itself have been mixed. But a professional journalist, with practiced eye, is bowled over by what has been done.

An adviser in California became the object of a suit by a local anti-smut group because of a series of articles in the school newspaper investigating birth control.

Underground newspapers flourished in such strangely disparate places as New York City, the state of Wisconsin, the megalopolis of Los Angeles, and Middle Illlinois.

A school paper in California led a boycott against a concert paid for by student funds but scheduled by administrators without consulting students.

The mayor of New York asserted at one time that the radical school press was one reason for unrest in New York City schools.

Changes in the school press. But not without controversy. The controversy was reflected by letters in *Revelation Now*. One student editor wrote in to express her problems and pleaded for suggestions and help:

DECEMBER, 1969

VOLUME 1, NUMBER 3

THIRTY-FIVE CENT'

A National High School
Journalism Review

THE DRAFT DILEMMA

Draft-card burning, anti-draft demonstrations, war protestors—all are evidence of a widespread dissatisfaction with the draft. In response to those actions, national leaders are now advocating changes in the Selective Service system.

The program presently being discussed as an alternative to the current draft is a lottery system in which those drafted would be selected at random. Former President Johnson advocated this system during his term of office.

The main advantage of a lottery system, according to Senator Edward Kennedy, another major advocate of the plan, is that it would eliminate the inequities of the present draft.

Under the present Selective Service system, those who register for the draft who plan on going to either college or vocational schools are deferred, or made less liable to the draft.

Those supporting changes in the draft system claim this provision is unfair, because it makes those able to continue their education privileged citizens. The high proportion of lower income group draftees illustrates this point.

Choosing draftees by chance would eliminate this inequity, lottery advocates claim. For example, one version of the lottery system would have all those born on a certain date drafted together, the dates chosen at random, perhaps by a computer.

Another feature of most lottery plans is that the present "old first" rule would be replaced by a "younger-first" method of selection. This would eliminate the uncertainty present when young men do not know whether they will be drafted until they are 26, the age at which the likelihood of their being drafted ends.

One disadvantage to this idea is that older youths, now deferred, would escape the draft entirely. Those opposed to the lottery plan also feel that a lottery would not be able to select those who are most fit for military training or highly skilled enough for present military needs.

Humphrey backs lottery

Former Vice President Hubert H. Humphrey has long advocated a lotter-type draft system in which only nineteen year olds would be called to military service.

In an exclusive interview with *Revelation Now*, the former Vice President said that he feels that the present draft system is, "filled with inequities and is an undesirable burden for our young people." Mr. Humphrey expressed the feeling that the lottery system would be beneficial not only to young people but to our entire society.

Humphrey, the unsuccessful 1968 Democratic Presidential candidate, remarked of the proposed new system, "The new system would permit our young people to plan their lives without constant concern of the Selective Service. They will know at age nineteen whether or not they will have to face the draft."

Mr. Humphrey, who is now a political science professor at the University of Minnesota and Macalaster College, agrees with President Nixon's methods of handling the draft problem, especially in the case of General Hershey. He feels that the decision to replace Hershey as head of the Selective Service was a good move. "General Hershey served a long time, and there was need of a new man," Humphrey concluded.

Student views mixed

The following opinions are those of high school and college students from around the country concerning the present Selective Service system and the new lottery proposal of drafting only 19 year olds.

Present draft

"I am against the present draft system. There are too many inequities in it, because the people who can afford to go to college can avoid the draft, but there are lots of people who can't afford it."

"I think the draft is good. I think men should have to serve in a war if it involves the U. S."

"The draft disrupts a young man's life and future by keeping him guessing from ages 18 to 30."

"Too many kids hide in colleges to avoid the draft. Get them out and make room for students who right now can't get into our colleges."

"This draft is okay in wartime, but in times of peace, no one should be drafted."

"I don't agree with the draft at all. If someone wants to volunteer his life for his country, it's fantastic; but if not, he should not be forced to. Forget the draft and start a volunteer army."

"The draft system isn't fair because black and white men, poor and rich men are not treated alike."

"The present system is unfair. You are
(Continued on page two)

Proposed draft

"The lottery would be bad news for my town. About 95 per cent of my school will go on to college, and many to graduate school."

"I don't want any draft at all, but I think a lottery is a lot fairer than what we have now."

"By the time a guy is 21, he no longer would have hard feelings against the draft because he would be out of its reach."

"I'd rather have a lottery. At least you have a better chance of legally escaping it. Also, you know how to plan your future."

"I believe that a 19-year-old is not old enough to fight in a war since he is not old enough to vote for the people who make the policies."

"I think that the lottery plan is ideal in time of war, but when no war is going on (if ever), I think that a voluntary army should be formed."

"The lottery doesn't give exemptions to married men, students, and others who are now deferred."

"Just forget the whole thing and form a voluntary army."

"The new proposal removes the uncertainty
(Continued on page two)

Inside...

* An in-depth story on how high school journalists throughout America covered the October 15 Viet Nam Moratorium.
* Words of wisdom from Chicago's Mayor Daley.
* Chicago: Demonstration Center of the World.

Dr. Thomson: 'white students must take initiative'

"I will give personal attention to any case of faculty racism I encounter," said Dr. Scott D. Thomson, superintendent.

"This school has been lagging behind in human relations and we ought to do something about it. One of the best things we can do is get Negro teachers. We're going to start recruiting in October.

"However, the students have a greater responsibility than the faculty in this area. Every time a committee is appointed, the chairman should make sure there are Negroes on it. Club officers should make a point of inviting blacks into their clubs. "White students have to take the initiative."

Dr. Thomson feels that racial relations is an important priority this year. Another is emphasizing the independence of the four schools. "I want to get away from the bigness of this school," he says. "If you don't, it becomes kind of a human factory."

He feels that ETHS "is in the forefront. Many schools are talking about the multi-school idea, but we're the first ones to have it going.

"Nobody knows how it'll work. It's never been tried before. We'll probab-

ly go through two or three years of evolution."

Dr. Thomson wants to improve communication between the administration and students. "I'll be meeting with individual students quite a bit. Anytime a student wants to come in and talk to me, he can. This way I can stay informed.

"However, I want the students to think of their school principals as their principals. I want them to be the leaders of the schools, not me."

Dr. Thomson would like to see the modular schedule used to greatest advantage, through improved use of independent study. "Independent study will become the main place to get information. The student will get more information through TV, films, slides, and tapes." He hopes that through all these programs ETHS will create more "positive people."

"We want better student identity, not just higher test scores."

EVANSTON TOWNSHIP HIGH SCHOOL, EVANSTON, ILL.

THE **Evanstonian**

Vol. 52 • No. 1   Thursday, Sept. 19, 1968

Dr. Thomson: "This school has been lagging behind in human relations and we ought to do something about it."

Adams: 'Blacks aren't freaks'

"I'd like to see less discipline this year. They should eliminate all these passes and nonsense," said Mary Adams, Bacon School senior and one of ten black students who discussed racial problems with Dr. Thomson last week.

Mary hopes that "restrictions will be lessened" during the coming year. "People should be able to walk in the halls of their own school," she says.

"I hate restrictions on dress and length of hair," says Mary, and she wants them changed. She also feels that "the assistant principal's role as disciplinarian of the school should be eliminated."

Mary is critical of human relations at ETHS. "Black people should not be treated as freaks," she says.

"Plays should be integrated, but not in the token way *Brigadoon* was. If you have one black lead, his opposite doesn't have to be black.

"It's unfair for a black person to go to a play and not see a character he can identify with. It's also unfair to black actors that they can't get cast because the community might not like it," Mary says.

"I'd like to see a renaissance of

school spirit," says Mary. "Too many people are not involved because being involved is not the 'in' thing to do."

She finds fault in the approach of the administration to black problems. "They tend to ask a few individuals what the problems are. The great majority of black students don't like being represented by one student."

She also feels student boards have failed. "If human relations councils would truly work toward helping people to understand people, they might accomplish something. If it's going to be a black-white clinic, it's not going to work.

"Human relations should be more of a natural thing," says Mary.

Mary is also concerned about student activities, particularly the senior class, for which she is a presidential candidate.

"The senior class should be a social thing," she says. "The main emphasis should be fun."

Mrs. Magett:
Human relations stresses respect, communications

"If I had one objective for my job this year, it would be that people would come a little closer to looking at each other as people. I would hope that they could find respect for each other on a human level," said Mrs. Dorothy Magett, co-ordinator of human relations.

"I don't want all white people to love all black people, or even all black people to love other black people. We can differ and still respect each other," she says.

Mrs. Magett feels that "it would be unusual if we didn't have some teachers here who are racist. I don't care if a teacher is a bigot, as long as he's a good teacher and can keep his feelings out of his relationships with kids.

"If a teacher can communicate to a student that he cares, nothing else is important." Mrs. Magett said that she firmly believes that the human relations program will help every teacher communicate better with every student, because if a teacher is bigoted and isn't relating well to black students, then he probably isn't relating well to white students either.

She hopes to change some attitudes and some methods. "You can't continue to do the same thing in the same way and not have kids rebel."

Mrs. Magett is also concerned with students' relations with students. "I'd like to see the students get to the point where they themselves can do the things they think adults aren't

doing. I'd like to see a disintegration of the fear between white and black students in this school, the fear of what friends will think, of what others will say.

"My final aim is for someone to tell me that they just don't need me any more; that ETHS doesn't need a human relations coordinator."

Anderson: 'Getting rid of suspension'

"I want to devote most of my time to getting rid of this system of just booting kids out all day. Suspension just hasn't accomplished anything,"

Mr. Anderson: "This year the students should take more power."

said Mr. Raymond Anderson, Beardsley School assistant principal.

"Right now it's kind of an endless thing. A guy gets thrown out of class for making noise and he's suspended for three days. When he comes back he's three more days behind and there's nothing left for him to do but make noise."

Mr. Anderson hopes to initiate after-school seminars for students who would normally be suspended, because a student in that situation "must be given a voice." He feels that these sessions would give students a chance to discuss their problems with the administration and he hopes to change some of the student's attitudes toward school.

"Waiting until after school would provide a cooling-off period. When he's mad and I'm mad it just ends up a shouting match and I win." Mr. Anderson is trying not to be over-

confident. "I don't expect the kid to change his mind the minute he leaves the room. I don't even know if this will work, but I can try it."

Mr. Anderson would also like to see a change in student responsibility. "Last year the students could have done 50 per cent more than they did in controlling the school, but they didn't want to pick up the ball.

"This year the students should take more power. They should be doing all their own monitoring of corridors and study halls.

"And they should change the clubs; these clubs have been here for years and years. We're a school with tremendous new ideas but the same old clubs.

"Students don't want to become involved, yet they're the quickest ones to say 'Why can't we do more?' The administration is waiting to hear what the students want to do, but the initiative for change must come from the students."

ISSUES AND PROBLEMS TO THE FRONT. Page 1 of The Evanstonian *is given completely to reports about issues, not about events. The issues-centered newspaper answering the WHY and HOW about news, instead of the event-centered newspaper answering who, what, when, and where. It was a radical departure for student journalism when the staff at Evanston Township High School, Illinois, took the step in 1968. On this first page of a new newspaper—three stories exploring the critical problem then of race relations in school, one story about the system of student suspensions and their relationship to "due process" guaranteed every citizen of the United States.*

In the main editorial for that issue, editors Jonathan Wolf and Gregg Borgeson explained their news philosophies. "Our news coverage will avoid the dull, straight story and replace it with in-depth analysis of major school issues and more enjoyable, humanized articles. We will not provide public relations for the high school, but rather will confront the problems of the school seriously and honestly."

On page 2 was a story about new modular scheduling. On page 3, a full-page story about students caught in the demonstrations in Chicago at the 1968 Democratic Presidential Convention.

The best editorial cartoon of the year was filed in the trash can. The cartoon depicted the Statue of Liberty with long hair, a beard and a clenched fist. Shame! . . . An editorial on the credibility gap between the administration and the students was censored because it contained "false information." There is no gap, said the principal, so the information must be false . . . being restrained to containing only copy which directly pertains to the school, we're limited. . . . The staff, including myself, is losing interest after three issues.

From Criteria of a Good Newspaper

Leadership—The newspaper shall act with courage in serving the public # Stimulate and vigorously support public officials, private groups, and individuals in crusades and campaigns to increase the good works and eliminate the bad in the community # Help to protect all rights and privileges guaranteed by law # Serve as a constructive critic of government at all levels, provide leadership for necessary reforms or innovations, and expose any misfeasance in office or any misuse of public power # Oppose demagogues and other selfish and unwholesome interests regardless of their size or influence. —From a committee of the Associated Press Managing Editors Association, 1962.

Even the professionals can sympathize with—and understand— those problems.

On the other side, there is Tom Brueggeman's ringing declaration of freedom as existent at Evanston.

But by encouraging its publication, the Evanston administration has shown true interest in journalistic freedom. . . . To be most effective as a force, the paper this year will use more of a magazine style approach to reporting, with many in-depth and feature stories. . . . *The Evanstonian* will run a front-page analysis story. . . . It will then follow up with an editorial on the subject. . . . *The Evanstonian* can only expect to do so if its reporting remains fair.

Well, it got to be well after 5 P.M. the day after Thanksgiving in Chicago, and the semicircle had grown a little, other students joining and wanting to know about *Revelation Now*. The conversation began to break down to little discussions. The interviewer left.

The next day the editors returned to Cincinnati, and Evanston, and Minneapolis.

Well, to be fair to teachers or advisers or administrators or so-called conservative editors or school boards, who are usually called the bad guys in controversies over what a school publication should cover—the problem is not censorship exactly. It is doubt—deeply set into public attitudes—about the purposes of education itself. Inculcation of tradition? Or freeing of the future from the past? Forcing students to conform to what has been—by time—tested and declared secure? Or releasing students to find new patterns, even though they may risk security or shake society and the nation? Or, in between those poles, where to? The purposes for schools have never been clarified successfully.

The problem resides somewhere in the response to a poll appearing in *Life* magazine, indicating that parents, for instance, tend to judge a school's effectiveness by measures of discipline. Not much room for the chaos of ideas and debate.

Caught in this paradox, many times between what the school would like to do and what it is expected to do, is the student editor. His newspaper is one of the few windows into the classroom and the school. Does the public really want to see that clearly into the classroom? Do school authorities want to allow that constant and unedited and frank exposure? Is it possible that student journalists can be trusted with that power of mirroring the school—correctly, honestly, truthfully? When must the window be draped shut for expediency to get a bond issue passed?

What about American society itself? It does not tolerate, and never has, a pure libertarianism, which student editors now call for as a right.

The school newspaper as a forum! Do readers really appreciate exposure to ideas other than their own? Should heretical and revolutionary thoughts be given the vehicle needed to ride roughshod over the status quo?

Also, there is that fundamental problem of a diverging lifestyle. Adults one way; many students another, ignoring the calls of adults to follow them. Robert Frost is taught heavily in high school, and one of his poems has tremendous impact on the young man—the poem about diverging roads:

> Two roads diverged in a wood, and I—
> I took the one less traveled by,
> And that has made all the difference.

Student response tends to be immediate and direct.

The student, free from worries about material security, is also more idealistic, he is a gambler, more impetuous. And so there is a gap in family and in school; one segment cautious and students more willful.

> Tell it like it is.
> Do your own thing.
> What's your bag?

Now, should student papers reflect this subculture, this road taken, less traveled by? Or should they reflect the more conservative attitudes, respect what is, and try to advocate the patterns of the system?

As one underground newspaper challenged:

We are a group of people who offer an alternative life-style to that of the establishment.

The school newspaper is right smack in the middle of a conflict extended to most areas of society. At the same time an editor who tries to serve faithfully and honestly can be caught between contrary forces. And so he must move with or against the propulsions of his own generation.

All of these questions, these counterattitudes, these pressures settle onto the student editor's shoulders as he tries to mark out a program for himself and his staff.

Result: in Stockton, California, a citizen group files a suit against the adviser of a paper for birth control articles. In a Reno high school, the principal says no to a Christmas issue that is to picture a black Santa Claus surrounded by children of many ethnic backgrounds. At University High in Chicago, the student council—in most schools a highly conservative group composed of "safe" students—cuts the funds of its own student newspaper because it broaches too many vital issues openly. The superintendent of schools for California advocates police searching student lockers and property for drugs.

In general, the student editor is saying more frequently in recent years—we are going to confront the issues no matter what happens. It is the only honest, intelligent decision—and the only one possibly bringing about the consensus that for 200 years has been the salvation of a comparatively free nation and people.

WHAT IS AN ISSUE OR PROBLEM?

Some news is centered on **events**—basketball game, student government meeting, speech, demonstration by students. Some news is centered on **persons**—interview with unusual hobbyist, profile sketch of person behind the news, press conference, human interest story about a person caught up in the news (as disaster victim). Some news is centered on **specific opinions**—editorials, interview with right-wing anti-sex-education leader.

Some news, in a sense broader and deeper, is centered on controversy, on confrontations of ideas and opinions, on problems unresolved in the community, on changes in society, on where mankind is going and where he has been. **Issues and problems.**

For instance:

The National Crime Commission in 1969 warned that American cities were well on their way to becoming places of terror and fortresses. WHY? How did this come about? What are the contributing factors? What are the possible solutions? What has been tried, will be tried, should be tried? What are some case studies—some actual examples and illustrations—of the fortress city? All of this goes into a problem-centered story. No one event, or one interview, or one idea, or one specific opinion, but many events, and people, and opinions, and circumstances—all explored and brought out in one story.

First, for the issue-centered story: identification of the issue or problem—and not always those negative in values. You start, as in the scientific method, with a hypothesis. *Newsweek,* for a story about the New Mood on Campus, worked from this thesis:

The mood of the American campus is apparently undergoing a striking change [in late 1969], militancy and violence are in good measure giving way to passivity and personal introspection, and the revolutionary impulse seems—for the while, at least—to have largely spent itself.

A **problem-centered story** begins with a concept, or a question —especially if journalism is concerned with change and crusade, not so much with reaffirming the status quo. One columnist, for instance, has pointed out that for conservative, 18th-century political philosopher Edmund Burke, "Half the battle was lost once that tiresome Jeremy Bentham got men to go around asking questions. Why is that lass hung for theft of a handkerchief? And why is that duke not jailed for theft of a country?" (Paul A. Samuelson in *Newsweek*.)

Such stories largely originate with editors who use "creative thinking" to pose such questions as:

√ What kind of freshmen do we have this year, and how will they direct or redirect this institution in the next few years? Who can give us this insight?

√ Seems to me there are an awful lot of policemen *visible* in school, on campus now, compared to a few years ago. Do the facts bear this out? If so, how did this come about? Why? To accomplish what end—REALLY: The questions are endless here. What effect on students, on the tradition of an open campus free for all ideas?

√ Conservative groups are more militant this year than the left-wing groups? Better check it out.

√ All the attention about curriculum has been put on Black Studies programs—are there other significant, even sweeping, curriculum changes under way, but overshadowed by the emotional Black Studies issue?

√ News note: Seven Ohio school systems face closing because of temporary bankruptcy. Better check the possibilities here. Or if we face no problem, what distinguishes us from those failures?

√ An ombudsman on campus—a place for students to lodge complaints and hope for some resolution. But the question is not who he is, or what he is doing, but WHY? Why, now, an ombudsman? A changing emotional climate? Severe student pressures? Liberalized administration? Just what?

√ Ralph Nader, the muckraker of the 1960's and 1970's, said students should worry as much about the violence he claims is being waged against the American consumer as about violence in Vietnam. A story there?

√ Student protests are lodged mostly in October and April and May. What are the determining factors here?

√ Suddenly, student momentum switches from Vietnam to pollution? WHY? A personal factor? Or a switch encouraged by subtle opinion manipulation? One national official has said: "The kids are looking for a new issue after Vietnam and this is it."

Once an issue-centered story has been identified, blocked out in

> What do we want to know?
> Who has what we want to know?
> How do we get it from them?

final stories may range from a one-article approach covering 15 to 20 column inches, to detailed stories spreading across one page, to a full package of stories filling a full, several-paged special supplement.

To Do, to Read, to Think About

1. Analyze the news possibilities of homecoming as an event: report of parade winners, interview with queen, summary of football game. Analyze homecoming as a source of issues and problems: interference with education, unusual tensions for football players, exorbitant cost of floats and dances. Look at other "news events" on campus for (1) event-centered stories and (2) problem-centered stories.

2. Some newspaper staffs work mostly with event-centered

news; others with problem-centered news. What would be the differences in attitudes of the staff, interest responses of readers, and reactions of the school community toward the two? Which to you would be the most effective newspaper? How could a newspaper become both event- and problem-centered?

3. For the results of problems investigated in depth read such books as *Children in Trouble: A National Scandal,* by Howard James (McKay). *The Battle for Morningside Heights: Why Students Rebel,* by Roger Kahn (Morrow Publishing, 1969). Ralph Nader's series of reports about environmental problems.

4. Some magazines have specialized in problem-centered reporting: *Harper's, Ramparts, Scanlan's, Moneysworth.* Some are self-disciplined; others tend to overstatement, exaggeration, and sensationalism. Look into some of the investigative reports in those magazines. Another: *The Washington Monthly.*

5. Begin to list in your pocket notebook (Future Book) problems and issues as you note them in the school and community (short lunch hours vs. etiquette and healthful eating habits; the concept of free education vs. the multiplicity of fees now to be paid; the high cost of graduation from school). Such ideas will get you started on issue-centered stories.

6. For one idea for a problem-centered story, decide who would be opposed to its publication—and why? And for whose benefit—if any—the story must be reported and printed? Would anyone or any institution be seriously injured by the story? If so, would the story be worth doing?

7. For stories about problems within journalism itself, try to get copies of such self-critical publications as the *Columbia Journalism Review, The Chicago Journalism Review,* any such publications in metropolitan communities in your general region.

8. Prepare an editorial of about 600 words to explain to the readers of your publication that you intend to switch from event-centered stories to problem-centered stories. Try to prepare them for the sudden change; try to anticipate their first opposition and persuade them to back you in your plans.

9. For national and state problems and issues, try to find "local angles"—that is, how they affect your students. National draft lottery? It must involve some of your students 18 and over!

10. Apply the same thinking about issues in the news to sports on campus: drinking restrictions, coaches' rules, pressures of winning. Also examine popular culture: as Vice-President Spiro T. Agnew in 1970 challenged certain lyrics of rock music as maliciously selling the drug culture.

11. What is "managed debate," "managed dissent?"

12. Evaluate the objectives of education in your community. Discipline? Learning to think and to defend ideas? Mastering factual material? Learning to live in an open society? Becoming adjusted to the prevailing system?

13. For one event—say, graduation—what stories can you think of that are

(1) event-centered
(2) person-centered
(3) opinion-centered
(4) problem-centered.

SOME FINAL IDEAS FOR DEPTH STORIES

Check the SOCIAL aspects of student life.

1. What social order in college will replace fraternities and sororities if they continue to lose power and prestige?

2. What is student response to (women's liberation movement, coeducational dormitories)?

3. Is there in the school any power ladder of administration, faculty, students, service personnel? Where does the student fit?

4. What about equality in the school?

Check the BUSINESS and INDUSTRIAL and ECONOMIC for story ideas.

1. What students are on the economic borderline of educa-

tion; that is, any increased costs would force them out of school?

2. Do students as consumers need more practical studies about such areas as real estate, investment, insurance, mortgages, and so on?

3. How much has education as a business displaced in our school systems education as education?

4. What are current student attitudes toward capitalism, the business ethic, industrialization?

5. How much do students and the school mean to the community's economy?

Check these areas, too, for depth stories:

1. HISTORICAL—The 10th, 25th, 100th anniversary of the school. The historical background to changing curriculums, enrollment, regulations, costs.

2. LOCALITY and PLACE—Local reactions to state and national news. Elections. New laws as they affect students directly. Social movements in the community as they draw support, opposition, or other reactions from students. Almost any news event outside the campus has some application *to* the campus.

3. ETHNICS—Racism and prejudice on campus. What the school does for deprived and underprivileged citizens. Ethnic mixture of the student body.

4. THE SYMBOLS—Current slogans and sayings. Fads and fashions. New forms of recreation or release.

5. NEW ON CAMPUS—Effects of, reasons for, responses to new religion center. Special classrooms. Teachers. Transfer students.

Ask yourself why? . . .

The need for dress code . . . suspension rules . . . run for student office?

Ask yourself about . . . student as an investor . . . new hobbies . . . student as politician or political activist.

Periodically, put together a column of comments and miscellaneous information and anecdotes under kicker headline:

Notes from the History Department

and so on . . .

Can you brainstorm five human interest depth stories?

And above all, be sure to study the investigative techniques used by the Ralph Nader Summer Study Teams in reporting the Food and Drug Administration, air pollution, water pollution. Here is the best investigative reporting underway today. The Reports are published by Grossmann Publishers in paperback and cost but 95 cents each.

Other Books by the Author, Bill Ward

Newspapering, a Guidebook to Better Student Publications, revised 1971; NSPA, 18 Journalism Bldg., U. of Minnesota, Minneapolis, Minnesota; $2.50, paperbound.
The Student Journalist Series (Richards Rosen Press):
   Creative Writing; revised 1971; $3.99
   Editorial Leadership; $3.99
   Writing Editorials; $3.99
   Thinking Editorials; $3.99
   Designing the Opinion Pages; $3.99
   Common Story Assignments; $5.79.
The Student Press 1971, an annual review of scholastic journalism (Richards Rosen Press):
   The Student Press, 1972; $12.50
Writing in Journalism, released in mid-1972 by NSPA (see above).

Additional Recommended Readings

About depth reporting: *Depth Reporting,* by Neal Copple; Prentice-Hall (Professor Copple is dean of the School of Journalism at the University of Nebraska which has developed an outstanding curriculum based upon depth reporting; students there produce several in-depth publications each year as part of classwork) . . . *The New Front Page,* by John Hohenberg; Columbia U. Press.

Depth stories which have been republished in book form: *The Bridge,* by Gay Talese (included in the collection *Fame and Obscurity,* by Talese; World Publishing Co.) . . . *The Shook-up Generation,* by Harrison Salisbury (about teenage gangs—older book but excellent reportage) . . . *Mississippi Notebook,* and *we are the people our parents warned us against* both by Nicholas von Hoffman (first from David White Co., second from Quadrangle Books) . . . *The Algiers Motel Incident,* by novelist-journalist John Hersey; Knopf (his account of *Hiroshima* may be first great depth report) . . . several books about the killings of students at Kent State Univeristy, especially *Confrontation at Kent State,* by Joe Eszterhas and Michael D. Roberts; Dodd, Mead & Co.; others by James Michener and I. F. Stone . . . See a card catalog for books by such depth reporters as David Halberstam, Jules Witcover, Clark Mohlenhoff, Nick Kotz, Fred J. Cook . . . See film libraries for "CBS Reports," "See It Now," and other television documentaries, especially "Hunger in America" and "Harvest of Shame."

"Depth" photography: see published collections about specific topics by David Douglas Duncan, W. Eugene Smith, Ken Heyman, Alfred Eisenstaedt, Margaret Bourke White, Emil Schulthess.

Best journals to read: The Wall Street Journal, The National Observer, National Geographic, Harper's, The Washington Monthly.